BILL KNAPP

Remember Who You Are

The Birth of a Young Man

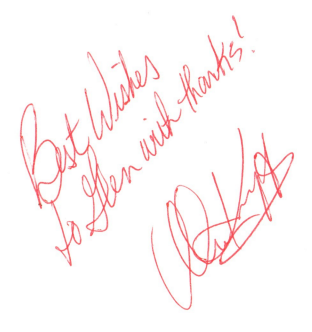

Copyright 2021

All rights reserved. This book or any portion thereof may not be reproduced or used in any manner whatsoever without the express written permission of the publisher except for the use of brief quotations in a book review.

ISBN: 978-1-09838-001-4 (print)
ISBN: 978-1-09838-002-1 (eBook)

AUTHOR'S NOTE

This novel has been many years in the making. It has been written several times and thought about constantly. You may wonder why a man in his 70th year would write about the life of a young man in his teens. It is, on the surface, a good question, however, my hope is that as you read the book you begin to identify with the main character, or even just a piece of him, realizing that at any age certain things are common in our hearts. In these early, formative years, every aspect of our participation in life is intense because much of it is being experienced for the first time. During this time in our life, we are so curious and so full of wonder. We see everything for what it means personally. That doesn't mean we are self-centered in an egotistical way, necessarily. It means we are on a constant search to find where we fit, whether it's within our family, our social associations or even with the world at large.

The participation in life's evolution from child to adult is so very influential in making us who we will become. Unfortunately, we don't have a chance to choose the place from which we start this adventure. It's how we interact and react to our lot in life that is important. Perhaps even more important are the people that influence us and directly or indirectly guide us through.

This book is not to impress or depress anyone or gain any kind of literary stature. It's a simple story, written by an ordinary man. I merely want to share some of my thoughts and life experiences in the hope that you understand, because you feel or have felt some of these things yourself in one way or another. I seem to remember these times in my life even more vividly than I do about the things that happened yesterday or a couple hours ago. (although that is more a geriatric condition)

During my years as an elementary school teacher, I read a rough, condensed version of this story to my class every year. It was an attempt to identify with them originally and to my delight and slight surprise they responded quite positively and always wanted to hear more. That reassured me that I was on the right track. Whether it was approved by administration or not, I didn't care. I read it to them anyway. I disguised it as the listening component of the English program, complete with tests and quizzes on the content. But invariably students would ask questions and want to discuss other more consequential, poignant things, things about their personal lives. At times they would corner me in the school hallway or while I was supervising in the schoolyard and tell me about what they were going through in their lives involving family or other relationships. I believe this novel had a lot to do with their willingness to open up to me. They knew that part of the story could have been about them and to them that meant I could understand their circumstances and that I would take them seriously. Now, years later (I don't want to say how many) I realize that maybe I can still reach people or touch them in some way, whether they are a teenager, or a fossil like me.

In an effort to appeal to both the younger set and the more mature reader, I have tried to describe things as if I were looking back explaining things to you. I have not, of course, been a part of all the events in this book in real life. Those things I have not been involved in I have experienced second-hand from others, mostly students of mine. Though the scenes and thoughts are being experienced by younger people, I have tried to describe them the way I would now to concisely relate to all ages. Any conversations between the characters are rendered the way I feel they would have talked at their ages.

Whether you are young or old, I hope there is something here for you. In fact, one of the main inspirations for this book was my grandfather, and he would be over 130 years old if alive today!

He gave me the title for this book as you will soon find out when you read on. Even if you regard it as just an amusing story or light entertainment, I would be happy. Perhaps it will jar loose a memory long forgotten. Perhaps it will bring a tear or a giggle. Maybe your child or your parent might find it identifiable, even moving. Please enjoy, and feel free to give me feedback through social media or any way you like.

CHAPTER ONE

To a young boy in his fifteenth year, Saturdays usually meant freedom. Joey wasn't suffering the drudgery of the 9 to 5 work week as yet nor did he ever envision a life of manual labour as his lifelong calling. It was not that he felt superior to those relegated to the mundane regime of that sort of lifestyle, there was just something else burning deep within that seemed to cry for the pursuit of a more creative future. Nonetheless, Saturdays were days when he could usually find at least some time to do what he wanted to. There was no formal structure to these days and more notably, no school. Perhaps, even more conspicuously, the reason these days had a certain laissez faire atmosphere was because Joey's father was away at work in the city. He could escape confrontations with him and with his older sister, Pam, on these days.

For Joey, the late spring was always the best time of year in the so-dubbed "Lake District" in which he lived. There were no tourists to speak of yet, the sights and smells of the pine forest and the sound of the lapping of the still frigid water along the rocky shores recently freed from the grip of the winter ice had an undeniably soothing effect on one's psyche. The sun's increasing strength kindled thoughts of summer and a fervency for favorable days ahead.

These days provided opportunity for hikes behind the house and along the shoreline with Joey's beloved Bernese Mountain Dog, Harriet. Joey knew the woods and the well-worn paths like the veritable back of his hand. He would stop every once in a while at a log or large granite boulder and swivel his flat top guitar around to practice a few chord progressions or even offer an impromptu vocal while Harriet would curl up contentedly at his feet or scamper and splash in the shallow water at the shore. Some days when the lake was calm, he would row out in his old leaky rowboat he had stashed in a miniature beach along his trail, and explore the coastline or catch a bass or two. To Joey, this was life the way it was intended. The music seemed to take him away to daydreams of performing for appreciative... no, adoring audiences where he was valued and genuinely loved. The pine scent, the angular beams of sun shafting through the trees and the tranquility of the gentle sounds of nature uninterrupted by humanity melded into Joey's concert hall where the entire natural world gave him a standing ovation. An escape from a challenging family life and a reincarnation from is gawky tall-for-his-age teenage frame.

As Joey sat slouched on the side steps of their rundown lakeside bungalow recalling these pleasing thoughts, it evoked the recollection of how it was Gramps who had given him his guitar last April for his birthday. That thought took him even further into his state of reverie and the most sacred of times for Joey. These were the wonderful outings spent with Gramps at the trout hole on Black Creek not far from Gramps' house just south of town. Yes, Saturdays could be so amazing when the weather and all the other conditions fell into place. For Joey all the stars had to align perfectly for him to have a positive day and this was not to be one of those days.

Joey's judgment seemed always in question by adults and in the last few months it felt to him like his opinions were not given much respect. Today he was destined to begin piano lessons, something he had been dreading since he conceded the idea to his mother a couple weeks ago but not before expressing his reticence. It would mean driving to the city in the embarrassing garbage-can-on-wheels his mother drove and succumbing to the tedious study of musical theory or "ants on a page" as Joey thought of it. This would be valuable time away from the things he held so dear on well aligned Saturdays. Being in public also meant more attention to grooming and proper attire. Being a skinny kid with blossoming acne and a stubborn dirty brown double crown made him rather self-conscious. It usually took copious amounts of water to "glue" down the horns atop his coffee-tinged haystack. The zits just seemed to come and go, first erupting like little sores he popped, leaving red wounds usually around his snout. In general, his burgeoning physical appearance was not much of a confidence builder which brought about a noticeable lack of poise and courage. Clothing was yet another issue. Jeans and a t-shirt or hoodie with old running shoes suited him best. His continual growth spirts, and scrawny frame meant that sleeves and pants were too short and there didn't seem to be enough holes in his belt for adequate suspension. He thought he looked like a snake he had seen on a nature show shedding its skin. Joey's mood slipped further into sullen doldrums as he waited for his mother to get herself ready for the drive to the city.

His disposition was broken briefly as he glanced down at his faithful companion, Harriet, who was returning his stare with her goofy grin. Her upper lip would often get wedged up over her teeth revealing a farcical expression as a result of an under bite she had since birth. Her defect was one of the main reasons they were able to purchase such a pedigreed dog because the breeder was unable to show her. But this so-called flaw also contributed to her sweet personality. The physical imperfection did not have any effect on the delightful character that almost all Bernese Mountain Dogs seem to possess. In fact, her clown-like expressions often provided moments of comic relief. Joey suppressed an urge to laugh out loud as he scratched her head affectionately. At moments like this she was his angel of mercy. She was his spirit guide from the astral plane stimulating an inner warmth and unconditional love. Most days it was difficult for Joey to absorb these feelings from the aura of his normal environment.

The muffled sounds of his mother rummaging around in the laundry room behind him brought him back abruptly to his current dilemma...piano lessons. He couldn't really say no to her because he was keenly aware of the financial sacrifice she would have to make to enroll him in these hideous lessons. Joey loved his mother dearly and understood her intentions were out of devotion to him and there were few people in this world as loving to him. But why piano? In Joey's limited grasp of the world, piano lessons were reserved for girls and the gentile artsy fartsy types. He pictured the stereotypical piano lesson candidate as a bespectacled briefcase-wielding intellectual, so easily identifiable. The words nerd, geek and dork came to his mind. These people were the targets, the bully magnets, the ones with the pudding dripping from their heads in the school cafeteria. There were many things in Joey's life he agonized about, and this was just something else. Truthfully, Joey was mostly worried that his arch enemy, Paul Sinclair and his band of brainless disciples would get wind of this and the personal assaults would begin.

After about a half hour drive out of their little town of William's Glen, they came to the larger more sophisticated town of Montrose. Everybody just called it, "the city". Along the maple treed avenues lined, one after the other with identical brick buildings seemingly joined together, they finally arrived on a quiet street presided over by parking meters. Joey's mom handed him some change, he reluctantly exited and deposited the coins into the meter. She slid across the stained, partially tattered blue car seat and exited at the curbside. The driver's door had been seized up for over a month now.

The car was a relic from a happier time for his mother, a time of romance, an inspirational time for newlyweds. All was well. The car was itself a metaphor for her life in its appearance alone. Once iridescent, unblemished, and safe it was now marred by confrontations and weathered by years of neglect and abuse. Hank and Joan Burgess were married in 2000 and bought the 1999 Chevrolet when Hank landed a good paying job in a flourishing auto plant in Montrose. What transpired after that was steady regression; a relationship doomed by alcohol and irresponsibility.

"Mom, is there any way we can forget this and maybe try something else?" Joey groaned as they walked up the sidewalk.

Joey glanced over at his mother as she seemed to be searching for words and struggling to stifle her aggravation while emitting an elongated breath.

Then, before he could foresee his own regret, he added, "I just don't see what piano and music theory have to do with just expressing myself with my guitar. What does some white-haired old bimbo know about guitar?"

Touching his arm and stopping she turned abruptly and said, "Joey, you have no idea, do you? You don't know Mrs. Greer and you don't know how old she is. You need to start realizing just who we are trying to help here. You need training and understanding of music if you want to be successful in the future."

Joey lost her after the first couple of words. They'd been through this before. As she continued he caught some of the more significant and emphasized words such as: "cost, music theory, your teacher says, your benefit, etc." but Joey was gone. He was fishing with Gramps and romping with Harriet back at the lake.

They continued walking up the sidewalk and a very pretty girl about Joey's age passed by and his thoughts were brusquely suspended. Joey was selfishly infuriated that he was tagging along with his mother, particularly at this moment. She walked by and they caught each other's look and he was taken by her alluring face. It seemed to him like she wasn't really walking. Her lissome figure was more floating past him. Her medium-length, tightly curled auburn hair bounced in front of a pair of intensely blue eyes. His heart rate quickened, he felt his temperature rise and his face flush while embarrassment overwhelmed him. He was sure his fly was down and he'd forgotten to put on underwear. Unquestionably the quick flash of her smile was derisive and insincere, he thought. Girls were beginning to have a strange effect on him and stirring up peculiar cravings that were somehow not always displeasing. The last few years of Joey's life had been so engulfed in insecurity and brooding mood swings that most of the time he felt somehow vulnerable and self-conscious, as if there was always something very inadequate about his appearance or the way he carried himself. He marveled at how the simple exchange of glances with a girl could have such a distracting and carnal effect on him. If a 10 foot grizzly was chasing him armed with a bazooka it would probably have had less influence than this one girl. How he wished SHE was teaching piano!

Joey and his mom turned onto the sidewalk and into the front yard of a large three story yellow brick row house. Joey could not understand why anyone would want to live in a house that was fastened to another and another for a full block; a very foreign concept to a small lake town boy. Each house had its own false peak and personalized entranceway. It was a beautiful sunny day, the air fresh and fragrant with the birth of spring flowers. Two small squares of grass were dissected by a perfectly level sidewalk edged precisely along both sides. There was not a weed to be seen and the grass looked too perfect to be walked on. Mrs. Greer had distinguished her portico with large privets on each side of the steps partially hiding the four white cement columns that spiraled up to support the porch roof. The wrought iron railings were painted red to match the door with its large brass knocker. The slat wood floor was gleaming with a fresh veneer of grey paint. At the top of the steps Joey noticed a girl sitting in a matching Adirondack chair who was no doubt another prospective student of Mrs. Greer's. Joey's inner self let out a sigh as this stereotypical piano student's appearance was clearly authenticated complete with glasses, tidy braided hair and a shiny chrome smile. To Joey, this humanoid was more an alien and he couldn't help wondering how his mother could possibly think he would fit into this scenario. Nevertheless, he smiled back congenially while his mom tapped the knocker.

Joey faced his mother as they waited to give her his most heartfelt look, beseeching her to change her mind. She returned a very unsatisfying vacant look that reduced Joey to an object as if he was another chair on the porch. Just as he had tuned her out earlier, she had now returned the courtesy.

Muffled footsteps and conversation gave way to the sound of the deadbolt turning and the grinding latch as the great crimson door swung open. The three women; Mrs. Greer, Mom and he assumed the tinsel faced girl's mom exchanged pleasantries.

The girl's mom reached out her hand saying, "Let's go dear. Goodbye Mrs. Greer, Mrs. Burgess."

Framed in the wide aperture of the entrance, an attractive woman of about 40 smiled genuinely and greeted them enthusiastically offering them her hand. Joan and Joey exchanged handshakes with her and entered her house.

She was not at all what Joey expected nor was the home. This couldn't be Mrs. Greer. Joey marveled at how wrong preconception could be. She was not a tottery, old schoolmarm but a bona fide cougar as his less articulate friends from school might say. She had a vigorous, wholesome face and a radiant smile with vibrant hazel eyes framed by long flowing brunette hair centrally parted and draped over her shoulders. She wore white slacks with a striking soft lapis blue drape front sweater over a thin black inner shirt slightly V-necked. From a distance Joey thought she could easily pass for an archetypical high school girl if it weren't for the crow's feet that sprouted in the corners of her eyes when she smiled. So faultlessly groomed and clean, with an understated clean fragrance, he speculated that his mother may have felt the same twinge of self-consciousness he did.

Joan and Mrs. Greer or Carol as she had introduced herself, began the course of requisite small talk, Joey's eyes began to explore the large living room they were entering. He kicked off his seedy and somewhat odorous sneakers and left them on the mat in the front hallway and turned into the room. His eyes first met a small gauzy fir ball sitting daintily on a beige rug near the center of the room. Her dog, a Bichon Frise, was even well groomed and compared to

Harriet, extremely in control and placid. Joey had to consciously shake off the remembrance of where he had last seen Harriet and where he would have preferred to be. The room did not smell of lavender or fetid aging. It was not festooned with a myriad of crocheted doilies, dust covered knick knacks and mismatched antiques. It was not anything like his presumptions. The room was cheerful and airy with white framed floor length windows all letting the sunniness flow throughout. The ceiling, the bookcases and the fireplace mantle all beautifully fresh and white against the honey colored hardwood flooring. Naturally the gleaming ebony grand piano sat slightly protruding from the front corner of the room in a position of status propped open and awaiting potential.

Like a fish out of water, Joey felt incompatible with the lifestyle these surroundings represented. The room exuded prosperity, success, happiness, meticulous attention to cleanliness and elegance…all things foreign to him. Other than outdoor pastimes, Joey enjoyed expressing himself on his guitar and pencil sketching. Although he fantasized about being appreciated and a better life in general, piano was never in the picture or even in his passing thoughts. Perhaps if Mrs. Greer were teaching guitar or drawing, he could have had a more open mind. Ever since he had brought his guitar in to show Mrs.

Phelps, the music teacher at school, he had been told how much potential he had and how the right education and training was necessary. He was unable to make the correlation linking what he dreamt and aspired to be and piano lessons. Now, standing in this ostentatious room with all its refinements, he felt a surging longing to escape it completely.

Joey moved closer to the two adults engaged in talk about grading, scheduling times and fees.

He became an observer once again feeling helpless to control his own destiny, frustration welling. Mildly compliant minutes ago, Joey now felt like he could detonate any second and worked desperately to prevent an immature outburst. To mitigate his mood his mind returned to the wonderful warmth of Gramps' company on the banks of the trout stream with Harriet sprawled on her back spread-eagle beside him.

"Joey? ...Joseph!" His mother interrupted his fantasy abruptly in an uncharacteristic brusque voice.

Joey realized he had been miles away internally.

Returned to the hopeless situation at hand he responded reflexively, "Uh? What?"

"Joey, please don't say, 'What'! I expect better manners from you, especially in someone else's home." Joan responded with a hint of embarrassment. "We are concerned about your future even though you don't seem to be. We are trying to decide what is best for you! Mrs. Greer would like to ask you a few questions. Please be kind enough to stay with us here!"

Joey tried to save face but knew he sounded only more juvenile, "But Mom, you know how I feel about this!"

His mother's eyes replied, and he knew that he had better clam up quick for fear of eternal or at least an epoch of living hell.

"That's okay," Mrs. Greer interjected, "I understand a young man's apprehension about studying music, especially on a Saturday. I bet you would rather be surfing the internet or whatever you kids do on the weekends. I think, though, that everybody reaches a point where they become mature enough to set their sights on a realistic future for themselves."

Unwittingly she had put him down. In an instance there were a million negative feelings brooding in Joey. Surfing the internet! Their computer was so old that it took 10 minutes to boot up. They didn't have money for high-speed connections and mp3 players or cell phones or any gadgets most kids had. The reference to his immaturity and missing the mark so completely about his preferred weekend activities ignited a fire of contempt for her. She couldn't know anything about him! Joey's life and the teeter totter existence he lived in came to a massive crescendo in a mere nanosecond. None of the good, just the bad and the ugly screamed at him from the inferno in his brain. Something as trivial to most people as an opposition to taking piano lessons manifested itself instantly into a rage that mirrored his life as it had molded him: his pathetic, pitiful life; his dysfunctional family; the incapable position his stage in life put him in. The road he'd travelled to get to this point was not like most other kids. He carried his degraded condition so very close to the surface. He was like a case of nitroglycerin in a prairie schooner pulled by a team of horses along a rough trail in a wild west movie heading for that impending pothole, pushing him over the tolerance level.

"I don't want these damn piano lessons anyway!" he blurted.

"Joseph! Apologize!" Joan snapped angrily. Joey was already out the door.

Joey found himself on a wrought iron street bench between a row of maple trees knowing he was in trouble feeling both enraged and ashamed. He tried to imagine how his mom was going to smooth this out with Mrs. Greer.

She walked past him and he got up joining her lagging somewhat behind.

"I'm sorry, okay? That's just the way I feel. It wasn't my idea to come here!"

Stopping abruptly and turning toward Joey, Joan's face was a picture of dismay. Joey instantly felt repentant for his words and actions.

"Listen, alright? This isn't easy for me either, you know. Believe it or not you don't always know what's best for you even though you think you do. You WILL begin your lessons next Saturday. It's all set up. The first thing you will do is apologize and then you better just grin and bear it! Do you think that we have money just to throw around on something useless?

The rest of the walk to the car Joey felt too regretful to think of anything to say, feeling more like a prisoner being escorted unceremoniously back to a cell. He noted how much quicker this walk was than when they had arrived. Joey's pathetic disposition made it impossible to make eye contact with her. So many thoughts raced aimlessly through Joey's confused mind. He couldn't get a grasp on the idea that adults had to make decisions for him. He was, after all, a thinker...not a typical 14-and-a-half-year-old boy. The entire episode was a vignette of his life of turmoil and the negative drops in his life's bucket. He did understand about the money. How his mom made the money go as far as it did was always a mystery to him. He understood too, that his dad was drinking it away almost every evening.

Apart from the rattles and the porous muffler, it was a very silent and uncommunicative ride home. Neither even glanced over at the factory where Hank worked as they passed by. Joey's feelings of invisibility returned but he felt no urge to ask any questions as if somehow all would ease with the passing of the miles and time. He hoped that his mom would be more relaxed when they reached home so that she could deal with his dad when he arrived.

Things had been getting worse every day between his mom and dad. Hank's buddies from work would drop him off anytime between 6 pm and after midnight. He rarely spoke a congenial word to his dad at these times. Joey preferred to shut himself up in his bedroom but he couldn't shut out everything he heard.

As they pulled into the gravel driveway beside their bungalow Joey felt an intensifying surge of guilt for his actions in Montrose. With a quick glance at his mother sliding across the car seat, Joey noticed her smeared makeup and watery eyes. He thought of nothing appropriate to say and silently they went their separate ways.

CHAPTER TWO

Joey spent Sunday cleansing his mental pallet by roaming around the point of land behind his house and wistfully contemplating everything from the existence of God to, "How did these damn rocks get here?" That thought occurred to him immediately after skidding down a boulder into the shallow shoreline slightly skinning his calf and soaking his socks and shoes. Harriet was already down at the shore chasing minnows in the shallows and glanced up apparently only slightly bemused at her companion's plight. Joey felt slightly embarrassed despite the absence of any human company. But embarrassment came easy to him. He always felt a little inadequate like it was somehow his first reaction to everything. His perception of himself in the mirror or in photos was that of a gawky, skinny-legged teenager with the ever-present cow lick pointing skyward from his double crown. He licked it, greased it, brushed it until his scalp tingled and even tied a wet towel around his head but up popped his crown every time. His torso seemed too long and there had yet to be any real surge in musculature development. Joey thought his head was too small for the length of his body and his overall perception was that of an ungainly, awkward boy. He didn't perceive that some of the girls in his school thought differently. Yes there were those long skinny arms and legs and a thin body but there was also that dark complexion and long hair covering one eye slightly that was rather attractive to some. Unfortunately, his lack of self-confidence restricted his interaction with others. Without many friends to reassure him, he lived for the most part, alone. Despite all those negative feelings a good romp in the woods with Harriet replenished his spirituality giving him a temporary otherworldliness, an escape that provided sleep some nights.

Although there were many well-to-do residents in the "Lake District" area, his house was an older one-story cottage that people used to rent by the week for vacation. It was very cold in the winter because it wasn't insulated to be a year-round home. That's the very reason his parents were able to purchase it so cheaply a few years ago. The "handyman's special" as it was advertised, was still desperately needing a handyman even after the five years they had lived in it.

His two sisters, Pam and Jessie, bunked in the back room next to the bathroom. Joey's oldest sister Pam was sixteen going on twenty-five. She had come by that portrayal quite genuinely as she was called upon to be a mother to little Jessie in many ways. It wasn't because of his mom's negligence that this came to be. She had to clean up after their dad and the three kids, provide meals and look for work with a five-year-old demanding the attention that five-year-olds crave. Many mornings, more in the last few months than Joey cared to think, his mom was in no physical or emotional condition to do anything but sit at the kitchen table staring glassy eyed out the window. He deeply felt her distress but had no answer, only a fierce, empathetic understanding someone his age shouldn't have. The only thing to do for him was to look ahead and pretend things would get better. He was often tormented by the nagging feeling that this was only wishful thinking.

On a typical school morning, Joey would bring in the day's supply of firewood from the lean-to behind the house. With the spring days getting longer the wood pile became shorter foreshadowing lots of chopping ahead to replenish the stock. This time of year, was special because it gave Joey thoughts of the warmth to come and the days with Harriet along the shoreline of Skogie Lake and, of course, fishing in the trout stream with Gramps.

After throwing together a sandwich made up of whatever was left in the refrigerator he would head out on foot for school. Normally the walk would take about twenty minutes; however, his active imagination and sense of adventure meant that "normal" was not exactly an accurate representation of the myriad courses he might take. His hike was interrupted by the sights, sounds and smells of the area. At this time of year, it was as if the blossoming power of the sun was a catalyst that liberated new stimuli for the senses. The pines that not so long ago were covered in snow and encapsulated in frost by the frigid temperatures were now emitting a comforting aroma that conjured up soothing feelings. The early morning moisture glistened, and mist rose from the low, marshy areas along the lake. Pausing once in a while to sit, he felt the warmth of the sun on his butt and hands, absorbed by the granite outcroppings which forced the gravel road to meander around as it made its way toward town. It is a wonder Joey even made it to school on these days. The whirring and buzzing of insects and the warbles and chirps of birds not seen in several months, the earthy smell emulating from once frozen ground, the high-pitched croaking of young frogs, all the sights, sounds and feelings transported him briefly into an ethereal plane where he was free to do as he pleased. He became a part of his surroundings; an environment where he belonged, was appreciated, and accepted. These thoughts became so intense and surreal that his conscious mind awakened realizing that this voyage of the mind was not taking him down the path to school and the realities waiting there.

There were so many more distractions along the way. There was his only real friend Jug, who lived a short walk along the road. They would often meet up at Jug's house and travel in tandem from there. Jug's real name was Josh Parker. Jug was slightly shorter than Joey with freckles and hair even more unkempt. Jug was tagged with that nickname because of his rather hobo-like taste for clothing, as per the old Archie comic with the character known as Jughead. His clothing was really not a matter of preference but more a reflection of his economic status combined with a certain lack of dignity. Where Joey would try to mask his impoverished circumstances through proper grooming and tasteful matching, Jug seemed oblivious to his outward presentation. There was something about the synergy these two had. They often had an uncanny ability to find trouble; mostly boyish mischief, but sometimes they found themselves in more serious predicaments. There was the time they broke into the old Simpson cottage and smashed in some windows. It seemed harmless enough to the boys since the place had been deserted for years and there were hardly any windows with any glass left in them. As innocuous as their perception of the incident was, it proved difficult to explain to Joey's mom when Constable Percy taxied them home in his cruiser. Joey managed to hide an old cigar box full of hand-tied flies plundered from the otherwise fizzled adventure. Dad never found out about that little escapade. When it came to Joey's dad there would have been very little discussion and very likely dire consequences. Since that great fish-fly caper the two had kept their noses clean for some time.

Past Jug's house the gravel road joined the main paved road leading over the bridge of Black Creek and into town. The bridge spanned the clear, icy-cold water where it emptied on the north side into Skokie Lake. There were many forms of wildlife to see from the bridge and the clear water and lofty perch provided a bird's eye view of a variety of fish darting in and out of the shadows of the creek banks.

Over the bridge and a short distance into town the journey would turn right down a smaller paved road. Along the road was Gramps' senior residence, two blocks before school. Many mornings in the springtime Gramps would be out in the gardens puttering about. Joey, and many times both he and Jug, would stop if they saw him and talk with him for a few minutes before continuing to school. Sometimes Joey would even slip away during lunch periods and visit with him while finishing his sandwich on the picnic bench between the residence and the trout stream behind Gramps' place.

Gramps was always happy to see him, and Joey was always comforted by the ardent devotion he had for him. He felt uncommonly significant or special around his grandfather. Sometimes Jug would tease Joey about Gramps. He would say that he was losing it or senile because of all the philosophical and rather profound advice he would occasionally offer. Jug had a way of saying things that did not offend Joey. There were few people who could get away with such veiled remarks. It may have been that Joey was willing to jest with Jug because he could see truth in Gramps' words. Gramps was a well-respected man who once held an important position in this once bustling pulp and paper town. At one time, he was even the mayor and the president of William's Glenn Furniture, with many employees and associates. He had been a pilot in the war and was ever ready to spin a yarn about his countless endangerments should the right motivation present itself. Gramps stood a mere 5 foot 6 inches with a completely bald head, pince nez glasses and an increasingly stooped posture but he was a giant superhero to Joey. Joey recalled upon meeting one of Gramps' old employees as he reminisced, how every day Gramps would make it a point to visit every man in the factory. There were over three hundred workers and Gramps knew all of them and their families by name and was sure to make some kind of small talk with them all before noon! It was this bona fide concern for the welfare of others that Joey revered so fervently. In fact, several years after Gramps retired, he was asked back to resume his presidency on an interim basis until they found a suitable replacement when the incumbent had passed away. He was and continued to be a revered and respected man most vividly in the mind and heart of his anxious teenaged grandson.

Although Joey was not a strong academic student, he did tend to excel in artistic endeavors. He just seemed to be able to express what he saw either through visual art or music. He wasn't a gifted writer, and often struggled to write a succinct paragraph but when it came to lyrics for a song, he was quite capable. Many weekends and sometimes after school he would find himself sitting under the willow at the trout stream either strumming his guitar or sketching. He found it surprisingly easy to capture the water using pencil or pencil crayon. Even though many people thought water was the toughest thing of all to draw or paint it was somehow just part of Joey's spiritual being. The gnarly shape of a jack pine was a favorite tree. In his eyes and his heart nature was something relatable, something alive, something changing and never completely stagnant. It was like he was... primitive, perhaps unevolved. He reasoned that most things in nature are imperfect and asymmetrical and therefore anyone who observed his work couldn't view it as a violation. Joey marveled at how this one particular spot was never the same. Each day he found himself there the scene was different, not just seasonal differences but micro, involving all human senses including the heart. Sometimes the scene and the feeling associated with this place even changed while he was there. There was so much beauty. The dappled sunlight filtering through the fluttering leaves of the huge willow canopy and the constant burbling of the stream dancing over the rocky creek bed were not just peaceful but hypnotic. Perhaps the best part of this place was that it was so private. Rarely would anyone walk through here. Joey would purposely take slightly different routes just so a path would not develop. The peace, the inner warmth, the sanctity of this perfect place provided Joey with an escape or haven which comforted him when things got rough at home.

    Joey always tried to time it so that he arrived at his school locker before Paul Sinclair got to his. Sinclair's locker was only two doors down from Joey's and he was a known bully and Joey was one of his favorite targets. Joey tried to get the principal to move his locker but did not want to make his reason known for fear of possible backlash. Jug's was in a different hallway and they tried to get his locker moved closer to Joey's. Jug was also a target of Sinclair, but the boys reasoned that somehow there might be strength in numbers. The school administration would not make exceptions so stealth and timing seemed the best defense. Apparently, Joey needed to recalibrate his ETA because the unmistakable sound of Paul Sinclair's $300 shoes shuffle-flapped up behind him along with his requisite chanting of a popular song. It seemed that Sinclair needed to announce his presence to everyone whether outside, entering a classroom or strutting down a hallway just to make sure everyone knew they were in the presence of the illustrious Paul Sinclair! He had a way of making others feel small and somehow inconsequential. He was not even a good singer and his voice grated on Joey like nails on a chalkboard. Sinclair was just an inch or so shorter than Joey but much more filled out. He was a school athlete and footballer. He had a swagger and an air that Joey despised in people, the kind of person that just had to take over a room when he entered, no matter what was going on or what conversations were happening before he arrived. He had perfectly quaffed blond air, piercing blue eyes and the most fashionable clothes on the market.

"Hey, Joe-boy!" He belched it out so that everyone in the county could hear him. "Nice jeans, man. Did your mommy pick those up at the truck stop or the dollar store?"

"What the hell is that to you?" Joey could never think of a great comeback.

"WA WA WA WA. What's that shit head? You don't need those books do you Joe-boy? You don't actually read in your RETARD classes do you?" he sneered.

As Joey's core temperature began to climb a couple of Sinclair's buddies gathered around him for the show. This had the makings for a very long day! Internal temperatures were at a boil. It was confusing to him that any time he became upset this overwhelming hot sensation permeated his entire being. It was like he was in a cloud of super-heated steam that paralyzed his brain and made reason impossible.

"Why don't you just piss off!" another brilliant response.

He stared blankly into his locker rummaging around for absolutely nothing while tuning out Sinclair and his cronies' cheap shots. Joey thought about the name, Joe-boy. It made him feel less than a normal, capable human being, like a meager glimpse into the heart of a black slave from pre-civil war time. Joey wondered why being the junior ski instructor at Kamawog Lodge and having a father that owns half the properties around the lake gave him these innate rights.

Bubbling over, Joey blurted, "Listen pretty boy, why don't you and your goons go and count your daddy's money?" Joey felt suddenly much better after that. But not for long.

That had been a switch that Joey probably should not have flipped. It was like Sinclair had been detonated because his smug countenance turned to rage. His books smacked the floor echoing in the hallway as he closed in on Joey, fists clenched. Joey knew he had gone too far this time. He was outnumbered, out muscled and fully expected his life to end then and there. He closed his eyes and was saved! Mrs. Phelps rounded the corner behind Sinclair.

"Is there a problem here?" she asked sternly.

Sinclair turned, smiled and told her, "Oh no, nothing's wrong. We're just having a little talk."

As Sinclair's disciples faded off down the hall behind Mrs. Phelps deserting Sinclair, he did a quick about-face and fabricated a search through his locker for something important.

Mrs. Phelps, none-the-wiser, continued, "So Joey, how are the piano lessons going? Have you started at Mrs. Greer's yet?"

Geez, there it was! Everything exposed and right in front of Paul Sinclair of all people! Joey felt like mush, like it would be a good idea to lock himself inside his locker. Instead, he just stood there melting as a huge grin spread over Sinclair's face.

"Well, I don't really start until next Saturday, I think. I'm not sure I am going though. Joey tried desperately to muster some pride and composure.

Out of Mrs. Phelps sight, Sinclair was doubled over in restrained laughter, turning red like he was about to explode!

The 8:40 buzzer droned, and the halls quickly emptied.

"Well, I guess we had better get to class, eh boys?" said Mrs. Phelps.

"Right, bye." Joey answered, turned, and attempted to escape.

"Joseph?"

"yeah?... I mean, yes Mrs. Phelps?"

Joey liked Mrs. Phelps and really didn't know exactly why. Maybe it was because she seemed to care and value his potential. She was a small, absurdly well-dressed woman with short brown hair with some white strands. Her face was fine featured and sharp like a fox. (pun intended) There was a sense of energy about her. She wore a slimming turquoise woolen suit and white blouse with a silver treble clef broach draped just below her neck. As slight as she was, she had a somewhat severe aura about her. Nonetheless there was a twinkle in her chestnut eyes that talked on their own. They told Joey that she thought he was capable, and he felt that message piercing through her austere presence.

"I really hope you will give piano a fair chance. You show so much promise in music. When you brought your guitar in to show me, I was impressed. I know you just strummed a few chords, but I was impressed with your touch and sensitivity. It felt to me like your guitar speaks to you in some personal way."

Joey's guitar did speak to him and her words resonated clearly. The pure sound of a well plucked chord or even single string offered clarity in his life, like a bell in a foggy storm.

"Well, I guess. Yeah maybe." He stammered, then fled to the safety of his home room and sat there in a trance.

Joey was not fully cognizant of the first couple classes. His second period was a "Developing

Language" English class. It was clearly regarded as "special" with all the negative undertones understood by much of the student body. Joey was fairly sure Mrs. Crane wouldn't notice if he were a little out of it. Many of the kids in this class had major problems with just about everything. Typically, the class was far too overcrowded for any true individualized attention. Joey wondered when it was that he missed what he was supposed to know by this age. He was just not overly motivated to read or write. His outlet for his creativity was through music and art. He had heard through some school evaluations and discussions that he was deemed very right brained. The English component was supposed to be part of that, but it was still in its infancy in terms of Joey's creative evolution and just words without music seemed rather boring.

There was also the contradiction when it came to science class. If the left brain was the analytical and the methodical thinking part, why did a right brained kid like science? Chemistry was on tap third period and he got to sit at the lab table with Jug. That might have something to do with his fondness for this class. The events of earlier today were beginning to fade or more accurately were merely shelved for later access. Mr. Vanderloop was a pretty cool teacher. He loved to joke around, and classes were usually a lot of fun. Joey's more upbeat frame of mind became diminished as he glanced back and over a couple rows where Sinclair was enthroned with one of his slug friends. There was a rather sizable group sitting near the back that were his teammates on the football team. You could tell this because when there was a game out of town and they were allowed to miss school it seemed like the entire back section of the class was absent. Joey was sure he could hear more whispering than usual emanating from back there and he was sure they were planning something at his expense.

While Mr. Vanderloop was dancing around simulating an excited electron, Joey noticed Sinclair twisting his head around whispering and a guy to his left trying to hide a piece of paper that was being passed from desk to desk. Joey had a low confidence level at the best of time making him feel like a target in any social situation and sometimes even when no one was really paying any attention to him. Joey would often find himself reaching down to make sure his fly was up just walking down the sidewalk. His emotional state was becoming weaker as time went on. There were so many negative drops in his life's bucket and each day the bucket became harder to carry. He was sure that whatever was going on at the back of the classroom was to do with the incident earlier this morning. As it happens, this time his concerns were justified.

As he turned back to catch what Mr. V. was doing Joey's eyes caught Billie's and she seemed to project a little smile in his direction. Joey had always had a curiously warm feeling toward Billie and thought her beautiful. He felt an attraction, not a carnal allurement but more a pleasant, affable chemistry...a slight witticism by virtue of this particular setting. Her beauty was in her eyes; the twinkle and the empathetic acknowledgement that was emitted in a fraction of a second. It was not the color of her crystal blue eyes, but the sparkle and the quick squinch. Joey figured that some girls were more or less just to be looked at in a physical way whereas Billie was more than that. Any girl that would play baseball and wear, "Billie" on the sleeve of her ball jacket was kind of cool, especially when her real name was Catherine Magee.

She got her real name from her father, William Magee, who owned the Magee

Construction Company, responsible for most of the building in the area and even larger office buildings in neighboring cities. The Magee family was probably even better off than the Sinclairs and the two families were known to hang out together. Billie worked at Kamawog Lodge during the summer, and was acknowledged to be Paul Sinclair's girlfriend. This was a reason to probably not exchange too much pleasantry. Perhaps Billie WAS just eye candy.

At the last buzzer, Joey was presented with the reason for the covert exchanges during chemistry class. There taped slightly askew on his locker for all to see was a note with the heading, "Sign this if you think Joe-boy Burgess is gay," in bold black marker. Beneath the heading was a rough sketch of a stick figure in pink pencil crayon sitting at a piano with musical notes scattered around the perimeter of the sheet. Under that were hastily drawn uneven lines where basically all of the chemistry class signed their names, except Jug's, of course.

Jug met Joey on the steps as Joey exited and it did not take much scrutiny to notice the dour look on Joey's face.

"Hey Joe, who ran over your puppy man?"

"That damn Sinclair, I'd like to run over him or worse!"

Joey flashed the note just long enough for Jug to get the gist of the intent and tossed it into the garbage bin beside the steps.

To Joey's surprise Jug leaned over and fished it back out to examine it more closely. After pondering the crumpled paper for a few seconds Jug looked up and with a confident stance pushed the paper back at Joey.

"Yeah, so? You tryin' to rub my nose in it or somethin'? Joey snarled.

"Take a close look at the names, man."

Joey examined the note again. The only thing Joey could really see through his blurred anger was the word "gay" and a class full of names. He looked up again to Jug and noticing his impatience turned back to the page for a more deliberate inspection.

"Man, I knew you wouldn't sign it! So I have one friend. Looks to me like I got a whole lot more enemies!"

"Yeah Joe, you got a friend. How many friends do you think Sinclair has? Those names on the paper aren't his friends. I know some of those guys. I hear what they say behind his back. They are just scared that they will get banned from the big group. Hey bud, you should take another look at that list of names 'cause there's something else important."

Joey scanned the list of names for the third time a little puzzled at Jugs insinuation.

"Count 'em," Jug suggested.

"Why?"

"Because I happen to know there are 27 in that class. I remember because when the grades were posted in the hall last week after our test I thought I did pretty well being 10th out of 27."

Joey tapped the page with his index finger counting out loud.

"There are 24 names."

"Bingo! Who else did not sign it?"

"Billie! Holy crap!" Joey almost screamed it out.

"That's right Joe. I'm surprised I caught that before you. Looks like the joke is on Sinclair, the omnipotent one! His own girlfriend didn't even sign it. So I'm thinkin' even she knows he's an asshole, man. Either that or she has a crush on you. You better hope that Sinclair didn't notice that. If he did, your troubles might be just starting!"

CHAPTER THREE

A couple days later, it was Day Five in the school's six day school timetable which meant art class. Joey loved art, especially these days because the class was pencil sketching, Joey's specialty. He did not care for the history or particular artistic styles used by the great masters. All he wanted to do was draw and make his mark look like something. Fortunately, this semester was a more "hands on" class and that was right in Joey's wheelhouse. It was just an hour, but it was an hour when he was often lauded for his work. Being admired or commended for anything was an extremely rare event in Joey's life. It was a class where he felt like he was in the upper crust and not so much of an underling. He was not vain about his skill or proclaim his talent. Rather, he just produced nice work and he really did not think that he was exceptional in any way, just a little above average perhaps. His positivity came more from the reactions of his peers than Miss Peterson, his art teacher, although it certainly did feel good when she endorsed his efforts. It was more the other students' envious looks and the times they would ask him for help drawing a something, because that gave him a sense of being important, or at least more significant. He was needed at home but that was when there were chores to be done. It seemed to feel so much better when his fellow students needed him in an esteemed way.

Ironically, there were those in the class that given a different setting would have been siding with and kissing Paul Sinclair's butt.

Joey caught Billie settling into her desk, preparing her paper for today's class. He thought it best to avoid eye contact to today. To have the tension settle since the gay thing, it was probably wise to avoid throwing any more fuel on the fire. Avoidance had been successful the last couple of days.

Miss Peterson was a real free spirit. Perhaps all art teachers were, Joey pondered. She wore so many different colors and scarves that there didn't seem to be any discernable style. Joey was not sure if she had legs, because her body was covered either with gypsy-like dresses and skirts or baggy leggings. She had reddish hair and had a freckly, plump but kind face. She wore weird glasses with red frames and triangular-shaped lenses one day and then the next day they might be green frames with Lennon style lenses. She was a person that just stood out in a crowd by appearance alone. The strange part was her eclectic wardrobe seemed to work for her. It was not like she was making a statement. It was more that you just understood that is who she was. Another amusing feature unique to her was her chaotic and seemingly unorganized desk.

Art was an elective for Joey this year and it was satisfying to actually have a choice. Mrs. Peterson seemed to be interested in anything that was produced. It was as if your artistic output was something that really couldn't be wrong in any way. In her eyes art by definition was a external expression of the artist's inner feelings and awareness, so by definition could not be judged as something mistaken or done in error. Her judgements were often positive and encouraging with only rare mild critiquing on style and precision.

Joey didn't really know too many students in that class. That was just fine by Joey because the art environment here was like a bunker from the often-troublesome outside world. To him it was a place of comfort like being with Gramps at the trout stream. When he would attempt to reproduce something, it came from inside of him, from places he knew and cherished. He felt as close to those places as he could be and still be in school. Billie was the only one he had actually talked to much at all, but she was not exactly a buddy or anything.

Today's class was on landscapes. While Mrs. Peterson was showing slides of paintings done by some of the greats such as Claude Monet, Paul Cezanne and Vincent van Gogh, Joey was inside his head thinking about what he would draw. At one point he did notice a painting called, "the Parc Monceau" by Monet and was taken by its tranquility and his amazing use of light. But mostly he was self-absorbed and imagining his hallowed spot by the stream and how to create shadows with only a pencil.

With the class winding up, Joey found himself applying some finishing touches to his sketch, adding a few modifications so that it would not give away the location. He felt the glances and curiosity of the other students admiring his work. Mrs. Peterson had pointed out a few minutes earlier that he had really captured the essence of the flora in this area around town. She used other words beyond Joey's grasp like, quintessential and allurement but he figured it was all good. Words were not his strength.

As Joey was working quickly to finish up some texture and shading on a granite outcropping he was adding, he caught the scent of Billie's musky perfume or whatever it was that girls like her wore. She walked by Joey's desk and asked Mrs. Peterson to show her some techniques. Joey was not sure why he even noticed. There was just something about Billie lately he didn't understand...some sort of fascination foreign to him. Even though he really did not know anything about what kind of person she was, he continued to watch, and he felt like almost everything about her was somehow captivating. Her face, her dark shiny hair, the way she moved, her small almost mysterious figure...he pulled himself out of the daydream and refocused on the shading.

"Joe?"

"Yeah?"

Geez, there she was, big as life, standing beside his desk! He felt odd and his hands seemed suddenly sweaty.

"Holy crap!" Billie looked around afraid she was too loud. "You seriously did that just this period? You are s o o o o o talented! Geez, I wish I could draw like that!"

Trying to contain his blush, Joey mustered a meagre, "Thanks."

"Mrs. Peterson told me to come and have a look at yours because I am having a little trouble shading some shapes. I can see why! Do you mind?"

To Joey the feeling of being needed took on a whole new wonderful dimension.

"Uh, no, no, not at all. Have a look if you want. I wish I had a little more time, like another period or two." Joey was surprised at his composure relative to his current heart rate.

He wondered what was going on here. He was just talking to another student about art, nothing else. He could not find reason for his butterflies. It was like stage fright or the trepidation experienced making a class speech. Yet he gathered himself and made himself available.

She showed him her drawing. He perused it thoughtfully but did not feel like he should in any way judge it. He could see where she could make some changes, but he thought it wasn't all that bad. He secretly thought that she was not particularly talented in this particular skill, but it was a reasonable effort.

"That's not bad. Maybe I can help you a little. Just let me finish up a few things here and I'll come back and give you a hand."

"Awesome! Thanks a lot!"

"Ok, see you in a minute."

Joey was a little confused; nervous yet surprisingly comfortable talking to her. His propensity for anxiety kicked in briefly. Was this a setup? Would Sinclair come crashing through the door once he was back sitting with Billie? He was briefly balancing his feelings of stress between his fear of Sinclair and the nervousness about being with a girl he was weirdly attracted to. Another thought crossed his mind while he mindlessly finished his drawing. Maybe Billie and Sinclair weren't really a "thing". Maybe that was just wishful thinking on Sinclair's part? Or…maybe she was just a student, who happened to be a pretty girl, and wanted help with her art and there was absolutely no reason for paranoia. After about 30 seconds Joey finished his art and turned it in to Mrs. Peterson who was back helping another student.

Joey moved his stool back to Billie's desk.

"Wow, I thought you needed more time!" Billie said, surprised to see him so soon.

"Yeah, well, I couldn't really do everything I wanted on it this period anyway. So, I thought I might as well just leave it."

As they talked, Joey felt a strange calmness creep in. Where was this coming from? Joey showed her a few things he had discovered like using an eraser to blend, and how to flatten out the pencil for different effects. His nervousness had vanished, he reasoned, because he was talking about something he felt adequate in sharing. By the time the buzzer went they had made some significant improvements to her sketch.

Joey went back to his desk and gathered up his things while Billie turned in her art. On her way back she stopped and watched him fumbling under his desk for a runaway pencil.

"Hey, Joe…I really appreciate it. I think that's at least one grade up from where it was before you arrived on the scene. I know I couldn't have done anything like that without your help."

"No problem." That seemed like the coolest thing he could think of saying. "Besides, I kinda owe you one."

Puzzled, Billie replied, "What do you mean?"

"The other day…You know…Sinclair's little note…the one you did NOT sign?"

"Are you kidding? I don't know why so many go along with him. He can be such an ass sometimes. Anyway, I think you're okay Joe. Thanks again. I better get going. I have a math test next period. See you later."

"Sure, no problem. See ya."

A strange feeling enveloped Joey for the rest of the day. Jug wasn't at school today which is

probably a good thing. He would have had to explain why he was in this pensive, otherworldly mood. He was Aladdin as he seemed to arrive at Gramps' place on a magic carpet not remembering walking there.

Joey figured it was about time he and Gramps planned a little fishing. Trout season was opening next week and fishing for speckled trout was Gramps' specialty. Mostly, Joey just enjoyed spending time with Gramps.

Finding Gramps back by the shed, Gramps turned and faced Joey with a raised eyebrow. He smiled and recognized right away that Joey's day had been a little out of the ordinary. That was an understatement. It had been an exceptionally good day!

CHAPTER FOUR

"Hi Joey, that is not your usual walk or should I say, shuffle. What put the pillows under your feet today?"

"I guess I had kind of a good day," replied Joey, trying not to come across as too pumped.

"Well, give me a hand here will ya? I don't seem to be able to squeeze these darn pliers like I used to. Either that or they're making this wire stronger."

"Sure, Gramps." Joey snapped through the wire with little effort. He thought about how quickly Gramps seemed to be getting older. He had never really thought about that seriously, figuring that he would just always be vigorous and hardy. Because Gramps was such a strong personality in Joey's life it seemed to him like Gramps was just as strong physically.

"Looks like we should get a little fishin' in this weekend, eh Joey?" Gramps had a sense for what Joey was thinking and usually Joey did not have to ask.

Joey beamed briefly and then clouded over.

"Yeah, that would be great, but it will probably have to be Saturday morning though. Mom's making me show up at the piano teachers at two o'clock... Gramps, do you think piano lessons are so important? I don't really want to go."

Gramps pondered the question," Hmm, well I reckon your mother is tryin' to do what's best for you. You might never have thought this, but when your mom was your age, we didn't have the means to give her that kind of opportunity. It was only a few years after she was out of high school that I got a better job and our lives became easier, and by then she was out being independent. Opportunity is the right word, I think. She just wants you to have the opportunity. Lord knows she can't afford it. I would like to help her, but she won't let me, and this place is draining me anyway. Just try and see what happens. I remember she tried the same thing with Pammy a few years ago – dancin' lessons, wasn't it? After a few months she knew she wasn't cut out for dance, and convinced your mom to quit. I don't imagine your mom is still harpin' on Pammy about it is she?"

"No, I guess not," answered Joey.

"Of course," Gramps continued, "Pammy's probably more interested in boys and other stuff now."

Gramps had a way of putting everything into clearer focus. He hadn't said anything that Joey hadn't thought of, but it helped Joey to hear it from someone he trusted. His words seemed to give him a little more freedom, like there was a way out... eventually.

"Joey?"

"Yeah?" Jocy answered, rather startled.

"You got somethin' else on your mind?

Gramps put down the spool of wires, took the pliers out of Joey's hand and gestured toward the picnic bench. As Joey approached the picnic bench, he watched Gramps lock up the shed and return to sit with him. It looked to Joey like Gramps was almost losing his balance at times. He had seen adults with just a little too much alcohol walk almost like that but this was a little different. Gramps reached for the table part of the bench and swung a shaky leg over the seat to straddle it and face Joey.

"I know that things aren't gettin' any better at home for you and your sisters or your mom."

This conversation was one Joey did not want to have. His mom was Gramps' daughter, and he knew it bothered Gramps and pained him to see her unhappy. The other reason it bothered Joey to talk to Gramps about this was because he could not be perfectly honest with him. He couldn't bring himself to tell him all the lousy things he heard and saw almost every day. He couldn't tell him how Dad would slap Mom, Pam and him around, how he even caused bruises on Mom's face or how he would throw things in his fits of rage.

Joey waited for Gramps to continue. He was staring off toward the stream and seemed to be gathering up his thoughts.

"Sometimes a man feels like he's beaten, you know?"

"What d'ya mean?"

"Your dad was once a good man, and things weren't always like they are now. He knows he's not doin' a very good job at bein' a father...or a husband. I think he's hurtin' bad inside and confused. You would tell me if there is anything really bad going on, wouldn't you?"

Joey choked out a weak, "Yeah...sure."

Joey stared blankly into the grass and thought about what Gramps was trying to say. When he defended his father like that, he realized he actually hated his dad. He wondered why could he not just admit that he was having problems and do something about it, instead of pushing his family around?

"You do know what I mean, uh, Joey?"

"Yeah, I guess...yeah." But in many ways, he did not.

"You gotta just remember who you are."

There was the famous line. When there were no obvious answers to Joey, or anybody in the family, Gramps would just say, "Remember who you are." As near as Joey could figure out that just meant when you're faced with something you should look deeper inside yourself for the answers and be strong. Often Gramps would lightly pound his chest over his heart as he said it.

As Joey began his travels through his teenage years this saying wasn't nearly as comforting or amusing as it once was. When he actually thought about remembering who he was, it was just a brutal reminder of that very fact. He knew who he was. He was Joseph William Burgess, son of Hank and Lillian Burgess, brother to Pamela and Jessica Burgess. He basically lived in a shack. He ate canned beans at least three times a week. His father was a drunk who boiled over with rage and took it out on his family. Joey thought how he did not really need to know who he was any more clearly. He knew his mom was losing hope, and she always tried to cover for his dad and hide the evidence of his violence. He knew that Pam was likely over at her junky boyfriend's doing drugs half the time. He knew that he was being belittled and tormented at school regularly and never had decent clothes to wear. Then he thought about Billie and today in art class...

"Joey?"

"Yeah, Gramps?"

"You look a little spacey or somethin' today. You wanna talk about it?"

"Uh? Oh, just thinkin' about what you said, I guess."

Joey never ceased to be amazed at how Gramps could see through him.

"Somethin' happen at school today?" he added.

"No, not really. I had a pretty good day for a change, that's all."

Gramps continued his uncanny understanding. He had rare empathy and acumen for an older man.

"I didn't ask you if something went wrong today. I would bet you found a new friend, right? Who is she?"

Wow, Joey was stunned once again! He figured old people were wise and had many life experiences on which to draw but it felt like he was kind of emotionally naked in front of Gramps. It's not that he minded that, in fact, it was really consoling. Gramps' intuition lightened the encumbrance of having to explain his situation to someone who may or may not understand his personal issues.

"Geez, Gramps, how come you think you know everything?" Joey grinned.

"Ha, well you've been hangin' around this old guy for a long time. I reckon I know you about as good as anybody."

That was so true, and Joey knew from experience there was no use in pretending things around Gramps.

"Well, I guess I did kinda make a friend today. Her name is Billie, but her real name is Catherine Magee.'

"Big Willy Magee's little girl? I used to do some work for his old man years ago. I always respected that family. They never seemed to let their money go to their heads... So, you like her or what?"

Slightly blushing Joey answered, "Yeah, I guess. I just helped her out a bit in art class. That's all. I was sort of surprised at how nice she was. Usually, girls are not all that friendly with me."

"Hey, bud, a friend is a friend. It doesn't matter if they're wearing skirts or jeans. You know what I mean?"

Joey chuckled and didn't think it was necessary to explain that Billie was wearing Levi's today. He knew exactly what Gramps meant.

"I think I better get going, Gramps. See you about 8:30 Saturday, okay?"

"Okay, Joey, and just remember, eh?"

"Yeah, I know, just remember who I am."

Joey thought about their conversation all the way home. He speculated that he was likely blowing the whole thing about Billie way out of proportion. Maybe next time he saw her he would just be, "Joe-boy", the dork. There were other clouds hovering over Joey's head as he made his way up the road. There was something oddly curious about Gramps. The last few times he visited with him he seemed increasingly sentimental; something in the way he looked at Joey. Joey noticed Gramps appeared to have slightly watery eyes when he said goodbye to him. He wondered that maybe Gramps was really worried and maybe he knew more about Joey's home life. But there was something else, something he just could not put his finger on.

Joey remembered a time when Jug's sister Lydia leaked out that Jug had a crush on Mary Ellen Simpson. His whole family razzed him so much that he was anxious about going home after school. The thought made Joey realize how important Gramps was to him. When Joey confided in Gramps, he knew it was safe, but he just couldn't tell him how his daughter was being treated. He knew he would have to tell him sooner or later. He loved Gramps more than anything on earth. Walking up the winding road, a tightness seemed to radiate from his chest into his neck and eventually into his face and this time Joey's eyes were watering.

CHAPTER FIVE

Joey was propped up against the wall on his bed trying to stretch his fingers around some new chords. Gramps had given him an instruction book on guitar, and he was deliberately working his way down the chord chart found on the last page of the book. He was discovering that most songs were constructed with only four or five chords and some even less. Nevertheless, he found it enjoyable discovering new sounds and building little tunes.

Harriet rested her head on Joey's bed looking up at him with big, sad eyes. This meant she needed either food or a pee break. He got up and walked toward the kitchen and she led him to the screen door. After a couple minutes she scratched to be let in and she took her place, curled up on the kitchen floor where she could survey most of the house.

It was nearly 10 pm and Joey's energy level was beginning to fade. His dad was still not home, and Pam was out, like she was more and more every night. His mom and Jess were already in bed. As his eyelids began to slowly close, he heard a light knock on his door and slowly it creaked open. Barely revived from his near sleep he could make out the diminutive form of his little sister in the doorway.

Rubbing his tired eyes, he half whispered, "What are you doin' up?"

"I can't sleep. Can I listen to you play?"

He could tell she had been crying because her eyes were still a little moist and red from rubbing them. She was a freckled face little five-year-old with long scraggly brown hair that came down to the middle of her back. She stood with a pleading look with one hand on the doorknob and the other clutching a small pillow in her other, resplendent in her pink flannelette onesie.

"I guess so," Joey answered, and patted the bed beside him.

She scurried over and curled up around her pillow beside Joey with her little hand on Joey's leg. Her adoration of her big brother had always been quite obvious.

Joey continued to practice some chords and strum quietly while sneaking a peak at her face periodically. He noticed that her face was rather blush and her hair was knotted and tangled like she had been sleeping on it for some time. The fine frayed ends curled up and stuck to her cheeks and chin, damp and sweaty. Jess watched Joey's fingers with her big blue eyes and glanced up at him once in a while when Joey struggled and became frustrated because his fingers did not cooperate.

"Joe?"

"Shhh, Jess, I'm trying to concentrate."

"Can you play a song for me? Will you sing?"

"Not now Jess, Mom's sleepin'. I don't want to wake her up."

"Please, Joe...Just sing real quiet...Please!"

Joey thought for the most part that sisters were a bit of a bother, but he felt sorry for Jess for the cards she had been dealt. It was not her fault she had inherited this dysfunctional family. Besides, tonight she did not seem her mischievous little self. There was an expression of need in her eyes, a pleading look that heightened Joey's feeling of compassion. Joey thumbed through the song book and found a page that met his approval.

"Here, hold this so I can see it...and keep it still."

Her face lit up and she smiled and sat up with a cute look of anticipation. Joey sang a few verses of "Kumbaya" softly, and as he peaked over the book noticed her contentedly trying to form the words with her lilliputian lips. He felt somehow closer to her than ever and watched as the concerned, wanton look began to disappear from her face. Joey thought how anyone else listening to him sing this cornball song would probably laugh at him and make him feel like a geek. Right now, this little human was making him feel like a superhero, rescuing the beautiful girl from the clutches of an evil villain.

Then suddenly, the pleased demeanor drained from her face and she started to cry! Joey felt at a loss for what to do in this situation. He set the guitar down beside the cot as Jess wriggled her way closer burying her head into Joey's t-shirt. He held her but could not find the right words for the moment. He knew full well what was bothering her and thought there were probably no words that a five-year-old would find comforting. He just hugged her tightly and cradled the back of her head with his hand. He could feel her shrinking slightly from her distress as she began to breath more easily. Joey felt more bitterness and anger for his dad than he had ever felt.

It was close to midnight before Joey realized that they had been asleep for some time. Jess was still locked to him, but she was fast asleep with her mouth open and breathing contentedly. He reached under her legs and struggled to his feet to carry her to her room. As he laid her in the bottom bunk and covered her up, he noticed that Pam was still not home. Joey was sure Jess would have no problem sleeping through the night now.

He reflected on how when Jess was up late, she could sleep through anything once she had really passed out. There were some confrontations at night between his dad, his mom and/or Pam that woke him, but Jess seemed to sleep right through. These conflicts were becoming more and more frequent.

Joey returned to his room, carefully closed the door quietly and curled up on the bed. He was now wide-awake laying there staring at the rips and stains in the wallpaper trying to remember who he was.

A few minutes later he heard a car pull up and a car door open through the guffaws of laughter, whoops, and four-letter word riddled utterances.

The car door slammed, and Joey could hear his dad yell, "Keep the shiny side up and greasy side down!" Hank squealed with hilarity, as if it was the funniest thing ever.

The car's engine thundered as it backed out spraying stones against their car as well as side of the house, only a wall's thickness from Joey's bed. Joey heard the unmistakable sound of a bottle breaking on the patio stones by the side door.

"Shit! My last damn beer!" Hank bellowed.

Joey knew his dad was pretty drunk. Nervously, he dug himself deeper into his thin mattress and felt sweat droplets trickle down his neck onto his shoulder. The spring on the door creaked as it opened and recoiled slamming it shut with a double whack. Joey hoped fervently that his dad would just settle down on the couch and watch TV or just pass out there.

Hank stumbled his way past the kitchen and into the back hallway. Joey tip-toed across the room and opened his door a crack. He could see his dad leaning against the door jam of their bedroom.

"C'mon Lil, for God's sake, it's Friday night! Let's go over to the Parker's and have some fun...Lilley? Don't ignore me, woman!" Hank's tone was abrasive and slurred, and his body rocked like he was trying to stay upright on a ship sailing in a rough sea.

"Hank, I'm tired. I really want to sleep." Lilley's voice was small and weak, and Joey could sense the fear he knew she was feeling.

Then came the thump of his mom's body hitting the floor. Hank's figure was no longer in the doorway. Joey turned away and put his back to the door as if the door was a barrier to the ugliness transpiring at the other end of the hall. He cringed with the sound of his mom's crying pleas echoing down the hall.

"Don't, Hank! Please...Hank...Don't!" Lilley's sobs grew louder, turning into loud cries. "No, no, no, Hank, please!"

Joey heard something crashing to the floor.

Hank began yelling, "Don't you think you should start being my wife again? I go to work every day to support you...and for what? This is my house, and you need to start respecting that. I am the boss here!"

There were ripping sounds and muffled thumps against the floor and more sobbing, "No, no no, please!", from Lilley.

Shaking, Joey grew more and more strained as the tears flowed. He could no longer remain on the outside. He needed to protect his mom. He squeezed the door handle, threw open the door and ran down the hall.

"Stop it! Stop it! Joey screamed through his tears, "Stop, Dad, please! Don't hurt her!"

Bursting into their bedroom, Joey jumped on his dad's back trying to pull him off his mother. The bedside table was tipped over and paper was strewn across the floor. The china lamp was in pieces and the shade crumpled by the struggle. There were sheets and blankets all over the floor and Lilley's flannel nightie was ripped and frayed. Lilly held her arms in front of her shielding her face with her hands and her chest with her forearms and elbows.

"What the hell are you doin' in here? Get back to your room and mind your own damn business!" Hank screamed as he shrugged Joey off against the dresser drawers.

"Stop it, stop it, stop it!" Joey screamed over and over in desperation.

Then Hank came at Joey. He looked like an enraged bull. His eyes looked glazed and possessed, his hair wet with sweat and drool dabbing the corners of his mouth like a sick horse. The mottled grey stubble on his face gave him the appearance of a crazed, unkempt bushman. Joey tried to scramble for the doorway, but Hank grabbed him by the ankle and brought him down with a thud. He stood up and dragged Joey by one foot down the hallway.

Joey could hear his mom faintly as she screamed, "Hank, don't hurt him! He's your son! Don't hurt him...I'll call the cops!"

Hank paid no attention to Lilley's panicked pleas. Joey could feel the bruising already starting on his buttocks. His head was bouncing on the floor and as he struggled to sit up Hank pulled harder, making his head crash back down. Joey's elbow slammed into the door frame of his bedroom, sending shocks of pain through his body. Hank reached down and grabbed one of Joey's arms and flung him onto his bed crashing against the wall and came at him again. Joey gasped to get his breath from the force of his back hitting the wall.

"Don't you ever come into our room again, you little bastard!" he raged.

Then he hurled the back of his hand against Joey's face. He felt a shock, a horrible dull thud and heard a sickening buzzing noise in his ears. Warm trickles of blood oozed from his nose and the warm liquid ran down into his mouth and onto his chin. The door echoed like a cannon as it slammed shut. Joey faded in and out of consciousness. Everything seemed to be spinning around and he couldn't get a full breath of air. He sat propped against the wall holding his head and his elbow at the same time. He gathered up the sheet and leaned his head on it, crying like he had never cried before. The internal agony in his heart was far worse than the pain in his head and elbow.

After what seemed like only a few seconds, Joey felt the warmth of his mom's arms around him, softly rocking him, holding him close, her hand gently stroking the back of his head.

"It's okay, Joey...It's okay...Just try to relax!" she whispered over and over.

Joey could feel his breathing gradually returning to a steady rhythm. He couldn't remember the last time she had held him like this. He thought how this was something he would never have felt comfortable with just a few hours ago. After all he was 14 and not a baby anymore. Right now, he wanted her there more than anything in the world!

She led Joey slowly to the bathroom. It seemed like he was stiff and sore everywhere on his body. Lilley gently swabbed his face with a washcloth and Joey could see in the mirror's reflection a cut on Lilley's lip. Noticing that made his eyes close and the tears come again. Lilley tightened her grip on his arm and put her other arm around his chest gently hugging him.

"It's okay, Joey. He passed out on the couch. He won't bother you anymore. He won't hurt us again. I promise you Joey! We will get through this. Things will get better. I promise you, Joey! I promise!"

In the morning, Joey heard his dad leave without a word. Joey listened as Lilley phoned Gramps and explained how Joey was a little under the weather this morning and that fishing would have to be postponed a few days. Then he heard her half-heartedly lecturing Pam about being out 'til three in the morning. Joey thought that his mom was probably glad that Pam had not been around last night to witness, and very likely participate in last night's mayhem. Lilley told Pam to look after Jess because she was going to the city for a while. Pam did not object or resist the directive in any way. She could see the cut and the bruises on her mom's face. She did not need Lilley to paint her the picture any more clearly. Joey listened as Pam and Jess began playing barbies in the lower bunk.

Joey got up and made himself some toast. He felt terrible! Every muscle in his body seemed to be screaming at him and he couldn't straighten his arm because of the swelling in his elbow. Harriet walked over and rested her chin on Joey's thigh, once again looking up with those big, sad brown eyes. Joey thought she might be comforting him somehow, but when the toast popped the reason for her attentiveness became obvious as she licked her lips and drooled on his jeans.

Lilly came through the kitchen giving him a kiss on the top of his head and a sympathetic smile as she headed for the door. She was all dressed up like she was going to a wedding or something, Joey thought. Her face was caked with makeup to cover last night's brutal inflictions.

"Where are you goin' Mom?" he asked.

"Into town for a while. You just rest. Take your guitar down to the river or out on the lake or something after a bit if you want."

It seemed to Joey that his mom was truly Gramps' daughter with the same insight and ability to know what he felt and what he needed.

"Joey?" She turned back to face him, standing in the doorway.

"Yeah?"

"Things are going to change. Please believe me!"

She turned, walked to the car and Joey walked to the front window to watch her driving off toward town. Somehow Joey knew this wasn't to be a shopping trip or a day of job hunting.

CHAPTER SIX

It was now Sunday and Joey's dad had not been around home for about a week. Pam, Jess and Joey were participating in a rare communal get-together around the kitchen table. Joey got up and was attempting to pry some burnt toast from the toaster. Both the girls were crunching away on some corn flakes while Harriet sat patiently waiting for an errant morsel.

Pam started poking at Joey by flashing a sly wink at Jess and revealed, "Did you know that Joey has a girlfriend, Jess?"

Jess' eyes lit up, "He does? What's her name? What's her name?" she asked excitedly.

They both found it hard to eat and tried not to slop milk on their chins as they started giggling at the thought of Joey with a girl.

"What do you know about anything anyway?" Joey reacted with a mild snarl.

"Well…" Pam was itching to continue. "Lisa told me that Cathy Magee told her that she liked you!"

"Joey's blushing! Joey's blushing!" chanted Jess.

"I'm not blushing…and people call her Billie not Cathy!" Joey blurted out.

Suddenly, Joey realized that he may just have admitted everything. In a desperate effort to recover Joey added, "Anyway, she's just a friend. I just try to help her out a bit in art class. You know... once in a while. That's all." Joey could actually feel that he WAS blushing now.

"Ohooooooooo," they both chanted in a discordant harmony.

"She's a girl, right?" Pam continued, taunting.

"And she's your friend, right, Joey?... So that makes her your girlfriend, right, Joey?" teased Jess as she spit milk all over the table in front of her while choking on her giggles.

That brought about more than just little teehees. They both became quite hysterical with a combination of belly laughs snorting and howls.

Joey had had enough. He left his toast on the counter walked briskly over to the closet, grabbed his fishing pole and tore out through the screen door to the echoes of two piglets squealing behind him.

Joey continued to Jug's place and the two headed out for the bridge like Tom Sawyer and Huckleberry Finn, poles in one hand and tackle boxes in the other. With the days warming the boys felt great to be outside in just jeans and t-shirts. They found themselves eventually on a large flat piece of granite on the shoreline of Skogie Lake where the stream emptied. There they cast their bobs into the quiet water and sat propped on elbows, faces in the sun. Each day the sun held a little more power, and the rocks absorbed a little more heat. What coolness came from the gentle drafts off the lake were tempered by the radiant heat under their bodies.

"Hey Joe," Jug interrupting the natural pleasures of the moment, "You know there's talk goin' on around school that you and Billie got somethin' goin' on."

"Seriously? You too? Jeez, c'mon. Give me a break!" Joey begged.

"Hey, I don't mean anything by it. It's none of my business really but maybe you need to think about this a little," Jug said more seriously.

"What's the big deal anyway. Can't a guy have a girl for a friend without everybody stickin' their noses in it. Soon it will be a headline in the town newspaper! It's not like I'm goin' out with her or anything!"

"Hey, you don't have to tell me anything if you don't want to," Jug replied looking a little hurt. "I just thought you should know somethin' about that. That's all."

"So, what's…what is the big deal?"

"Well, I told you, it's none of my business but…geez, Joe, if I've been hearin' things about you and Billie from other guys, don't you think that knob Sinclair is goin' to hear about it too? There are so many idiots that want to be his friend and … you know, get in tight with him and his crowd. I think half of his friends just want free stuff, like getting in some free skiing or a ride in one of his fancy boats. You know what I mean?"

"Yeah, I guess so," Joey admitted.

"I'm not sayin' you should be afraid of him, but you know how he is always braggin' about Billie bein' his girl and stuff."

"Okay, okay, I get the picture! So what am I supposed to do about it anyway?"

Jug gazed out over the sparkling lake bemuscd. "How the hell should I know? Maybe you should just make her not like you or somethin'. I'm just the guy that's warning you about trouble ahead. Sinclair has such a big frickin' ego and he would do anything to keep his big man reputation or popularity or whatever he thinks he has over the rest of us."

Joey was quite keenly aware of what Jug was trying to say. He thought how frustrating it was to be subordinate to someone just because he had money and material things. Joey turned his gaze to the lake and tried to find options to weigh. He pondered Jug's suggestion for several minutes. The more he thought about it the angrier he got. It was probably because his emotional state was not the healthiest lately. There was no way that self-centered, fat-head Sinclair was going to tell him who his friends could be!

"I won't do it!" Joey blurted out.

"Geez!" Jug jerked upright. "Are you trying to give me a heart attack?" Jug grabbed his chest in mock heart failure. "You won't do what?"

"I'm not goin' to dump friends just to please that dick!" Joey snarled.

Joey was determined now. He had heard stories about people that demanded respect because of their power and not their character and this thought came back to him now. He remembered a quote he had heard somewhere, "Don't desire respect, inspire respect."

"I don't think having money and toys deserves respect... unless you earn it by being a good person." Joey added.

"Yeah, I agree with you Joe. Well, you got more balls than I do then!" Jug answered, pulling up a little perch, unhooking it and plopping it back in the shallow water.

Joey was glad he had Jug to talk to. If he couldn't talk to him about his feelings, then who? He remembered Gramps at that moment. He probably could talk to Gramps but there was something about sharing things with a friend his age that seemed easier. He remembered Gramps saying, "A friend is a friend," after he had shared his story about Billie in art class.

"Yeah, I guess I really do like her," Joey admitted resolutely.

"I knew that," Jug nodded.

"How could you really know that?" Joey asked. He noted Jug's attention veering away from his fishing line and fixing his gaze further out into the lake.

"Look, man, I'm not blind, you know? I can see the look in your eyes every time you mention her and how you get all defensive when somebody teases you about her. And lately, well you have been sort of daydreaming lately…you know, like you're on Mars. Your body's here but your thoughts seem to be far away.

"Oh, is that right? And where and when did you get your PHD in psychology?" Joey quipped.

Jug got to his feet abruptly and started winding up his line. Then he bent down, put his hook and leader into his tackle box, snapped the lid shut and turned to walk back toward the bridge.

Joey realized that he had hurt Jug's feelings but didn't think he needed to be this touchy.

"Where the heck are you going? It's not your problem. You just goin' off poutin'?" Joey said regretting it instantly.

"Yeah, I guess so, Joe. Look, I know this thing with Billie must be kind of botherin' you whether you say so or not. I guess girlfriends are more important than your other friends sometimes. You are just not yourself these days. That's all I know. I hope you know what you are doin'. See ya later."

He took a few more steps toward the road.

"Jug?" Joey quickly raised his voice.

"What?" Jug answered, looking back halfheartedly over his shoulder and shrugging.

"C'mon, will ya? Come back over here and sit down…please? I'm sorry. Really…I mean it!"

Jug slowly pivoted around and found his way back to his place beside Joey on the rock. Joey began to realize what was upsetting Jug. He was right. He hadn't called on him or met him after school or any of the usual stuff for a few days. He recognized now that he had been pushing his best friend away. At that point Joey figured he needed to be straight with him, no matter how much it pained him to talk about it. Joey wound in his line and bounced the bob up the rock, setting his pole down and turned on his side to face him.

"Jug?" Joey said tentatively as if he wasn't sure how to go on.

"Yeah, what?" answered Jug, still maintaining a rather long face.

"Remember last week, when I told you how I got my black eye and my sore elbow?"

"Yeah, so you ran into some tree branch or somethin'. What about it?" still half looking the other way.

Joey looked down and tossed a pebble into the lake, "Well, I wasn't exactly telling you the truth."

Jug turned toward Joey looking him in the eye baffled.

"You know how Dad comes home late some nights and sometimes he is a little drunk from being out with his work buddies?"

"Yeah, I guess," Jug answered.

Then as Jug examined Joey's face more closely his own eyes widened. Joey knew then that Jug was understanding what he was trying to explain.

"Jesus, Joe! I had no idea things were THAT bad!"

They both simultaneously looked back toward the water, picked up their poles and resumed fishing. It was as if they were fishing for answers or what they could say next that would be of any consequence.

"Sorry, man. I just didn't know!"

"I know, Jug. Nothing is your fault. I have been holding it in too much and I didn't realize that I was affecting you. I know I have not been myself. I can't seem to figure out what I should do about it...as if I really have the power to do anything!"

"Where's your dad now? I just thought he was away workin' or somethin'."

"Mom says he's just gone away. I don't know where he is, and I don't know if she wants to talk about it or tell me. I'm not sure if the cops got him or what. I don't want to press her about it...you know? He was really crazy there last week! I mean, he really beat Mom and I up pretty bad. Mom says it's over, but I know she is hurting inside. You know what I mean? You understand?"

"Yeah, but damn, man, I wish you had told me sooner. That sure explains a lot about what's been goin' on with you!"

Joey was sharply aware now that Jug did understand. There was something incredibly special about that afternoon. He and Jug both knew that from that point on they would never doubt their friendship. They fished for another hour or so and when it became painfully obvious that fish would not be on either one of their menus tonight, they decided to go home and see what their refrigerators had to offer.

On the way back home, they stopped in front of Jug's place. Joey noticed that Jug had the old goofy glint back in his eye.

"So Whadya goin' to do about Billie then?" Jug asked.

"I'm not really sure yet."

"Well to me it seems like you want to be more than just friends but maybe that's all she wants. Who knows...girls!? If she is telling other people that she likes you, maybe it's more than that. If you are not going to just dump her or try to just be a friend, maybe you need to start makin' some moves, eh?"

"Make some moves? How am I supposed to do that?"

"You're the artist, man. Doesn't that mean you are creative? I guess you'll just have to use your imagination bro. I'll tell you one thing though. If she does like you as more than a friend and she doesn't think you like her like that, you might as well kiss her goodbye."

"How in the heck would you know stuff like that?" Joey answered, somewhat impressed at his friend's seemingly knew found wisdom.

"I saw a movie last night about that." Jug laughed. Then they both had a good chuckle and a snort or two.

"Hey, I'll work on it okay? Just don't push me. I'm still not really sure that she actually likes me...you know?"

CHAPTER SEVEN

It was day five at school and Joey was pumped. He was going to ask Billie to meet him somewhere, somehow! He still did not really understand his attraction to her. He definitely did not know what, how, or when he was going to say it, but he was convinced that he had to pull it off. This was such a foreign concept for Joey. Asking a girl to see him? How did this happen? As he lay in bed awake in the still early morning darkness, his mind felt like it was in overdrive. It seemed to Joey that life was becoming more and more complicated as he got older. He wondered if everyone had the same feelings as he did or was he the only one in the world that felt things this way? The turbulence associated with his family, his social life, his future, and just being a floundering zit-faced teenager, made focusing on what was important seemingly impossible.

This morning he paid a little more attention to his looks as he stared back at himself in the mirror. He wondered how anyone would find him attractive. At least there were no new zits. Every morning, there had seemed to be another one about to burst through the surface that needed popping. His hair had no real style and his mom only cut it when it got particularly unruly, but most of the time it just sat slightly above his right eye with the ever-present cow-lick at the back. Clothes were never purchased as a fashion statement but more for purpose, comfort and affordability. Jeans, t-shirts, flannel button-up plaid shirts, socks and underwear by the dozen, and as cheap as possible, were the standard shopping criteria. Even his voice that seemed to have changed into a more manly form lately, would occasionally rear its squeaky cherub side. Although he could usually control it, when he was particularly stressed or nervous, he had no idea what pitch would be emanated. Joey wondered if it was worth facing life some days but staying curled up in a ball in bed did not seem to be a great alternative. He thought, "I guess no one will ever find me very attractive if I stay in bed all day and don't give it a chance."

He grabbed his lunch made up the night before out of the fridge and headed out the door leaving the grating creak of the spring and the double smack of the screen door behind him. Harriet was right behind him. She had mastered the art of getting through the door just before it clapped shut while not running into Joey's feet. Disappointed that Joey was headed out the laneway and not back to the bush, she lay down with her front legs crossed at the end of the laneway projecting that doleful look that melted Joey every time.

"Bye little girl. I'll be back. Be a good girl now. We will go for a walk later."

He patted her head as she leaned into his hand lovingly, then gave in and rested her head down on her forelegs and followed him with her eyes as he walked away down the road.

There was no sign of life at Jug's as he walked by, so he continued and found himself walking by the old general store a good half an hour before he usually did. He realized that he hadn't even said goodbye to his mom or Jess. Lilley was back home getting ready to take Jess into the city. She told Joey she had, "meetings" to go to…whatever that meant. Joey had a snippet of understanding of what that implied, but really did not want to think of those things today. This morning he found himself walking faster than usual. He was even too early to catch Gramps out in the garden. He headed straight for school and sat perched on the large flat-topped newel post at one side of the old entrance to the school, rehearsing his approach to Billie. The old entrance was around back and was rarely used anymore. This was the best spot, since most people entered the school through the newer entrance on the other side of the school…a part of a big new addition a couple years ago. He could be relatively at peace here and avoid interactions with inquisitive peers.

Cars, trucks and buses motored by, birds tweeted, insects droned, a distance train horn blared. After a little while, the murmur and intermittent cackle of arriving students echoed from around the corner of the school. Joey sat detached from all that, fixed on his objective. He was playing out the scenario that awaited him. Should he appear confident, aloof, and cool? Should he be shy and quiet? He realized that he probably didn't have a choice on how to act because his natural awkward self would likely take over anyway. What were the exact words he should use? He found himself practicing out loud.

"Hi Billie. How's it goin'? How about you and me goin' for a picnic on Saturday?"

That sounded too direct. Maybe there should be a little small talk first.

"Hi Billie. Nice drawing you got goin' there. Wanna take a walk on Saturday and maybe do some sketches or somethin'?"

Nah, she probably wouldn't go for that, Joey speculated. Sketching would not likely be her idea of a fun afternoon.

"Hi Billie. What are you up to on Saturday? Think we could do something together?"

That sounded better but still kind of dumb to Joey. He wondered why he was so afraid of blowing this one little interaction. Of course, any time you do something for the first time it's challenging, he thought, and this was definitely the first time he'd ever asked a GIRL to hang with him. Chuckling to himself with a sneer, Joey theorized that maybe he would have asked a girl before if he thought they would actually want to be with him. Everything was so confusing! Life was so much simpler at Jess' age. Geez, he thought, what if she just flat out turned him down? What if she was already doing something with Sinclair? Suddenly he heard a familiar voice.

"I thought I'd find you around here. Man, you're early this mornin'! I'm guessin' this is art day, right?" Jug prodded in jest.

"Hi, Jug. Yeah, how'd you guess?"

"Stop worryin', man! If she likes you, she likes you. Don't get so uptight. Just be yourself or you will never know if she likes the real you."

Joey marveled at how good that felt. He was not sure if it was the words or just knowing there was a friend that had his back. He knew Jug's advice was solid and logical but that only slowed down the butterflies whirring around in his stomach a little bit.

Joey managed to avoid Sinclair for the morning and faked his presence through the first couple classes of the day. He was there, present and accounted for but his thoughts were a million miles away. When it came time for art he settled in and pretended to be intensely fixated on finishing up a project. He glanced up in time to see Billie coming up the aisle toward him on the way to her desk. Joey caught her eye and smiled and she smiled back. He suddenly felt a glowing, warm sensation like he was running a temperature and his vision blurred slightly.

" Hey, Joe. How ya doin'?"

"Oh, hey. Uh, good. How are you?" Joey replied as nonchalantly as possible.

"Oh, pretty good."

Billie didn't even really stop walking. She just continued to her desk and got her art stuff out. Joey was once again swimming in thought - mostly apprehension. Maybe he was moving too fast. Maybe he should just wait for another time. He thought of the disappointment Jug would lay on him. He thought about the long week that would go by before he would likely be this close to Billie. He knew he had to risk it today.

Miss Peterson spent almost the entire period showing slides of various artists' drawings which meant that there was little time to work on the projects in progress. Finally, they were given about fifteen minutes to draw. There didn't seem to be any logical reason for Joey to get up and go back to Billie's desk, but he was running out of time. He could not risk approaching her in the hallway. It had to be here, in this class, where the walls provided protection from Paul Sinclair. Before he knew it, the buzzer sounded, and everyone began charging out the door. It was now or never. Luckily, Billie was still gathering up her things back at her desk. Joey made his way back and pulled up a neighboring stool. She was slipping some papers into her portfolio when she looked over at Joey and smiled.

"Hey," Joey offered nervously.

"Hey again, Joe. You know, I'm gonna have to get a bigger folder or something. Things don't quite fit in here anymore."

"Billie...I was wondering...would you...I mean..." Joey let out an exasperated sigh and a little embarrassed giggle and shook his head with a smile.

"Sure, Joe. I assume you thought it would be cool to get together sometime?"

Joey was stunned. All he could do was laugh right out loud and Billie joined in with him.

"Yeah, I guess. How did you know that?" Joey answered sheepishly.

"Oh, a girl has her intuition as my mom would say. How about in the park beside my house on Saturday after lunch?" she flashed a coy smile at Joey.

"That was pretty bad, uh?" Joey smiled and continued shaking his head.

"Nah, I think it was kinda cute...I really got to get goin' though, okay? I'll see you Saturday?"

"Yeah, see ya Saturday!" Joey called after her.

There...it was done. Joey felt like that was a major milestone in his life's journey. He was actually going to have a rendezvous with a girl! It hadn't exactly been smooth, but the results were all that counted as far as he was concerned.

The roller coaster was at the top of the ride for Joey. Mom had postponed piano lessons for a while, since the events of the other night with his dad and Joey was a happy camper.

On the way home, Jug said he had to hurry and do some chores for his mom so Joey told him to go ahead and he would go see what Gramps was up to. He looked first in the vegetable garden where he usually found Gramps puttering around, but old Mr. Becker was the only one there, hoeing some weeds. He saw Joey and pointed toward the hammock draped between two trees on a row of maples on the other side of the tool shed. Joey caught sight of a figure slung inside the frilled canvas sheet with a straw hat tipped down over his face. He had never seen Gramps flaked out in the middle of the afternoon before. Joey walked gingerly toward the hammock clearing his throat in an attempt to get his attention. Gramps didn't budge.

"Gramps?' Joey said, quietly.

"Uh? oh, Joey, hi." He yawned and slowly moved himself into a sitting position balancing tediously.

Joey could not escape how stiff and fragile Gramps seemed to be getting. Gramps rocked the hammock to get himself into a standing position. He reached out for Joey and he gave him the crock of his good elbow for support. Gramps grabbed hold of it and slowly straightened his legs and then his back. They made their way over to the picnic bench and sat facing each other. Gramps still looked a little drowsy.

"Sorry, Joey. I guess I dozed off. Us old fogies are kinda like babies, eh? We need an afternoon nap once in a while."

"No prob, Gramps. It's a nice day and that hammock looks pretty comfy."

Joey noticed that Gramps was starting to revive somewhat but his eyes still looked tired and runny in the corners. Gramps grabbed the top of the picnic bench with shaky hands to adjust his position.

"Gramps, are you feelin' alright?"

"Oh, yeah, pretty good for an antique," he joked and smiled. Then, to divert attention from himself said, "I'm glad you came around today. I was hopin' we could talk some. Guess we haven't really got out fishin' yet since the season opened."

"Yeah, I know. But we will soon I hope."

Joey felt weirdly guilty, like he was supposed to initiate the idea for this Saturday. The way it usually worked was Gramps would phone and check it out with Joey's mom and then away they would go. Things seemed different now. Joey had an uneasy feeling that their afternoons hiking back to the trout stream may be slowly coming to an end. The exhilaration and optimism Joey experienced earlier was beginning to fade. No one meant more to him than Gramps. Joey sensed that there was something else Gramps wanted to say.

"Yeah, I guess we will soon," Gramps replied with noticeably less spark than usual. "So, how's it goin' with your new friend, Catherine, er I mean, Billie, isn't it?"

"Yeah, that's right. Ok, I guess. She seems like she will be a really good friend, Gramps."

"You know, Joey, you should take her to your spot back at the stream and show her how to catch some speckles or somethin'."

He turned to face Joey more directly and gave him one of his knowing little winks.

"Eh?" he added, slapping Joey's thigh in an attempt to tease.

"Yeah, maybe Gramps. That spot is kinda private though, you know?... Just between you and me? Jug doesn't even know about it."

"I know what you mean Joey, but I reckon that someday someone will share that with you other than just me. Sooner or later, you're goin' to have to let someone into that private world of yours. It won't be so bad for someone else to know more about your personal life. It can be helpful to have someone know what's important to you. When time goes on even some of the not-so-good things are important to share. That way you don't have to carry so much around yourself."

"Yeah, someday, Gramps."

Joey reflected quickly over Gramps' words. He couldn't shrug the thought that Gramps wouldn't always be around. It felt like Gramps was giving up and that soon he wasn't going to be able to share some of that precious, private world. Joey thought that Gramps might think that Billie or someone like her, would be special enough to share those things with. Right now, that idea seemed far away and Joey tried to ignore the idea of Gramps not being there.

"Joey, what I really want to say is, well, your mother and I have been talkin'. We just want you to know that things are goin' to work out okay, Joey."

"What have you and Mom been talkin' about, Gramps? What's really goin' on?" Joey asked, half hoping he wouldn't answer.

Gramps shifted his position and replied, "Well, that's up to your mom to tell you, all in good time. I'm not sure she knows exactly what's goin' on herself. Try not to concern yourself with that stuff. I know Hank's your dad and you got a right to know things, but there isn't that much to know yet. Your mom's worried about you. She's doin' her best to protect you kids and herself. You gotta trust her, Joey."

"Why do I have to be protected from my own father?" Joey felt the cherub's voice squeaking through. "We are his family! He should be protecting us! Why doesn't he just quit drinkin' and beatin' us and try to make things better?" Joey felt his heart rise in his chest and push out a tear that was wiped away angrily. A shaky old hand gently touched his thigh.

Joey had always wondered if Gramps was aware of the physical part of his dad's behavior, but his words reassured him that he knew everything. Joey realized it was a heavy burden for him to bear as well.

"It's going to take a little time, Joey. The only way I can explain it is that your father is sick and it's not the kind of sickness that you can just take a pill for. You just have to be as strong as you can. You gotta remember who you are more than ever."

Gramps lifted his hand and patted Joey's thigh to comfort him. Joey turned and saw the wetness in the old man's eyes. Gramps turned away slightly so as not to show Joey his pain, but it was too late.

Gramps swiveled on his seat and stared into the bush beyond the tool shed. "Life is hard sometimes, Joey. The only one you can count on in the long run, is yourself. If there are people in your life who can share the bad things, that really helps, but you're the one that can really deal with it or do something about it if you are able. Right now, we are all a little bit helpless. It's about shielding you kids and your mom from the bad things right now. Are you understanding, Joey?"

He turned and forced a half smile as he slapped Joey's leg and winced as he pulled himself to his feet.

"Yeah, I guess so," Joey answered faintly, looking downward.

"Well, I gotta get these old bones movin' over yonder to the garden before I seize up."

He disappeared into the shed and came out leaning on a rake.

"See ya, Gramps. I'll come by in a day or two."

"Do that. I don't figure on leavin' the country," Gramps replied jokingly. "Be good, eh?"

"Yeah."

Walking home alone, Joey felt amazed at how life could be so happy one minute then cruel and sad in the next. Gramps was sure right about life being hard sometimes. Joey thought how he contemplated things more deeply as the years went by. Some days it was difficult to imagine what the purpose for life really was. He couldn't really bring himself to believe in God and just go pray and make everything okay. Yet he knew there was something more to life than this. Maybe heaven and hell were right here on earth. He had heard people say, "Life is what you make it." If that were true, why did he feel so out of control over his own life? He didn't feel like he could make his life go one way or the other. Today he had been at the very top and the very bottom of his roller coaster.

CHAPTER EIGHT

Joey woke and rolled over to the gritty squeaking of the old springs in his bed. He thought he must have been tossing about for a while, because his t-shirt and underwear were soaked with sweat. The first thought that entered his mind was Billie. Sitting up, his bare feet resting on the worn and faded linoleum floor he snickered out loud. How could he feel so worked up over meeting with a girl? Hopefully, Billie would never know how much of mess his nerves were in. Logically, meeting with a friend should not cause such angst. Did that mean that he might be thinking of Billie as becoming something more than a friend? Joey questioned his sanity after that thought. The odds were so stacked against him…major obstacles… Paul Sinclair, the difference in their lifestyles, and his shortcomings such as intelligence and looks. He wasn't rich or smart. While he thought he may be okay looking, he wasn't sure how he could impress anyone with the clothes in his wardrobe. Any ensemble he could muster would still project the same seedy, meager presence.

Joey pulled himself out of this self-deprecating daydream. He decided that all the worry was unproductive, and the reason for it was the very fact that he didn't have that many friends. Because of that he thought he better be careful not to ruin whatever friendship he already had with her. Worrying... AGAIN?

Propped against the wall and staring up at the pines through his bedroom window, it seemed hours before the misty light turned blue between the branches. It was a warm morning for early June. He made his way to the bathroom, showered, and put on his best jeans (holey from wear, not style) and slipped on a clean t-shirt. After pouring himself a bowl of cereal, he sat at the kitchen table munching, his thoughts full of anticipation and hoping that today would be an "up" day.

"Hmm, showered and up for breakfast at seven thirty on a Saturday?" Joey's mom stood in the hall doorway in her nightgown. Harriet got up from her spot on the floor and came over to Lilley wagging her tail.

Lilley had once been a very attractive woman. She had a slender figure and mousy brown hair with big brown eyes and sharp facial features. There was latent beauty there, but she had let herself go somewhat. Her sadness often permeated her exterior and had manifested in premature wrinkles around her eyes and mouth. This was not lost on Joey. He was keenly aware of the price she had paid in the last couple of years.

"Yeah, hi mom. I thought I'd go for a walk, maybe get some fishin' in," Joey lied.

Lilley smiled and Joey knew he was beat. "Oh, and just what kind of fish are you after today?" she chuckled, raising her eyebrows.

"Okay, I'm meetin' Billie at the park after lunch."

"Billie? Oh, you mean Catherine Magee. Sounds interesting."

"Yeah, well, it beats piano lessons, and she hates the name Catherine, Mom. Billie is what her friends call her." Joey could feel himself becoming defensive. "And friends are all we are."

"Hey, down boy! I wasn't even teasing you, was I?"

"Maybe not, but I know what you were thinkin'. I've taken enough dissing from the girls already!"

Lilley pulled out a chair and sat across from Joey at the table. Harriet laid back down in resignation, realizing no food was coming her way at the moment.

"So, when are you meeting her?" Joey noticed a genuine sincerity in her voice.

"About one, I guess."

"Um...Don't you think you'll have to have another shower by then?" she grinned.

"I knew it! You just couldn't resist, could you?" Joey said, turning a little red.

Joey got up and stomped for the door.

"Hold it right there, young man!"

Joey could tell by the unusual emphasis in her voice that maybe he should do as she said and go sit back down. He slouched into the chair he had just vacated and turned to face the music. Lilley poured a cup of coffee, set it on the table and sat back down searching for Joey's eyes. Joey, arms folded, peeked up through his dark hair now covering his right eye. He noticed that her face was stern but with an empathic presence.

"You may not totally believe me, but I really was your age once upon a time! I just might know a little bit more about what you're feeling than you think. Sometimes you need to listen to people that have experiences you can learn from."

"Aw, Mom, geez!" Joey feigned severe boredom looking skyward and wishing he could be spared the impending lecture.

"Just listen for a minute, please. Then you can go and spend the day as you wish, okay?"

"Yeah, okay," Joey relented with a mild curiosity about what was coming next.

"I have two things to say to you. First, I think it is great that you have found a new friend and that you obviously think a lot of her. I sure hope that your expectations of this relationship will flower and become something great for you but don't rush it. Don't imagine too far down the road. You have only really just met her. I don't want you to get hurt. Understand?"

"Yeah, Mom. What else?"

"I also want you to know that when my business in the city is all cleared up, and I can get you there, I fully expect you to start those piano lessons. Is that clear?" Joey felt as though her eyes were burning right through his head.

"Yeah, yeah, okay!" Joey quickly blurted to shorten the discussion. "Can I go now?"

"Yes, you may go."

Joey got up and began rummaging around in the closet for his rod and tackle box. When he stood and turned around his mom was standing right beside him with Joey's guitar case in her hands. Harriet stood looking back and forth at the two of them. Lilley smiled and pushed the case toward Joey.

"What's that for?" Joey wondered, puzzled.

"Take it with you," she urged.

"Aw, Mom, everybody thinks I'm gay already!"

"Since when does a guitar put that label on someone? For lack of a better example, I bet people didn't think Johnny Cash was gay when he was seen carrying his guitar! Anyway, it doesn't matter what people think. You know how awful a gay person would feel if they thought that being gay was so horrible. You need to think about these things a little more. All I'm saying is, well, just play her a few chords or something."

Growing agitated, Joey added, "And then what, watch her throw up?"

"Joseph can you just once take a little advice from your mother. I was not only your age, but I was a girl your age. If someone thought enough to play his guitar just for me, it would be...well let's just say that gesture could replace an awful lot of words. Trust me, she will love it."

She winked and smiled lovingly at Joey while he thought it over. He grabbed it, juggling the rod and guitar case in one hand and the tackle box in the other and headed out for the trout stream, Harriet at his heals.

Joey knew he had lots of time, so he sat down on a big rock by the cedar tree in the front yard.

"Come here, girl."

Harriet obliged, tail wagging, looking up at Joey in what looked like a smile. Her tongue was hanging out and she was panting, almost like she was excited.

"Aw, little girl! You wanted to go for a hike, didn't you? Do you still love me?"

Joey pushed her away playfully and sensing this was play, Harriet bounded back and the two wrestled for a few minutes, happy in each other's company. Such a loyal friend, Joey thought. There was nothing ever angry or mean about her. All she knew was love. There was never any strings attached to that love either. No matter how hungry she was or how lonely, without fail she was always happy and ready to be Joey's friend. She reminded Joey of a conversation he had heard on TV.

A little girl who had just lost her dear golden retriever to old age was crying and upset. Her mother was consoling her as they sat on the front porch steps of their farmhouse.

The little girl looked up to her mom and said through teary eyes, "Mom, I know why dogs don't live as long as we do."

Her mom looked down kindly, "Why do you think that is, dear?"

"Because they don't need as much time as we do to learn how to be good and kind and loving!"

"Wow, you are so right, dear!" the mom admitted as she sweetly held her sad little girl.

Joey would never forget that sentiment, because Harriet was the absolute embodiment of that idea. If only all people could be just inherently good and kind no matter what their life dealt them, what a wonderful world it would be!

He felt embarrassed and his conscience-stricken teen brain made him feel awkward and a bit stupid to be carting all this stuff through town. Fortunately, it was early so he would not likely run into anyone of much consequence.

He spent the morning at his special place on the bank of the trout stream, wondering if Gramps and he would ever relive any of those wonderful times he had had there. This place was like a friend to Joey. The breeze was humming in the pines and the willow waved a "hello" to him. The smell, the sounds of the gurgling brook and the trickle of sunlight was magical, and it comforted him. This place was always there. It would not leave him. It always made him feel comfortable, accepted, and positive...like Harriet did.

He spent a little time casting. Looking under the tray in his tackle box to change lures he noticed a brown paper bag that was not there the last time he used it. He peaked inside...a sandwich! He felt a hollow swelling in his chest, a lump in his throat and emitting a little tear, realizing that his mom could also make him feel the same way this place did. He was sorry for the way he had spoken to her earlier, but also felt lucky to have her in his life.

Joey arrived at the park about fifteen minutes early. He could see Billie, already there, sitting on the bench facing the lake. He paused and looked down at his guitar case, and suddenly felt those nagging insecurities again. He wondered what people would think...a real lover-boy walking toward a girl in the park with a guitar in tow. Fortunately, he had stashed the pole and tackle box back at the fishing hole.

Billie, fixated on the shimmering water, did not see him coming up behind her. He paused to gather his composure and courage. She looked so beautiful to him in her blue shorts and blue and white striped t-shirt. Despite her rather skinny legs, there was a kind of athletic look to her. The sun was glistening off her long, shiny brown hair that had a freshly washed look... with the bounce you see on TV ads. She shook her head to shoo a fly away and that's when she noticed Joey. Joey made it look like he was looking around for her.

"Hey, it is you," Joey said.

"Hey Joe, c'mon over," she motioned with a wave.

Joey took a seat beside her and propped the guitar case on the bench on the side away from Billie to diminish its conspicuousness. But, of course, that didn't work.

"I'm glad you brought your guitar. You goin' to play for me later?"

"Oh, yeah, sure," he answered coolly.

It was as if she had the ability in thirty seconds to make him forget all his nervousness. He felt oddly at ease sitting there with her. They exchanged the obligatory small talk about the weather and how beautiful the lake looked. Joey was tempted to tell her how good she looked but could not muster the nerve. They talked about how the school year was almost over and the looming summer holidays. They found themselves talking about all sorts of things; people, and situations, laughing at some points and exaggerating the characteristics of teachers and friends. They both could feel the bond of friendship taking hold like they both hoped it would.

Billie got up and walked over to the shore, kicked off her tennis shoes and stood ankle deep in the still cool water, her feet sinking slightly in the red sand. Joey followed her and stood with her in his old crocks not worrying about removing them. They stood there side by side as Billie pointed out a small sailboat gliding silently out on the sparkly water.

"Hey, Joey, I got something I want to show you!"

To Joey's delight, she grabbed his hand and led him through some thick bushes where her property bordered the park. They found themselves in a small opening at a stony little beach.

"What do you think?" she asked enthusiastically, pointing to an old flat-bottomed rowboat pulled up under some willowy young trees.

"Wow! That's cool! Does it float?"

"Sure does. Dad gave it to me last year. Wanna go for a little ride?"

"Sure!" Joey was glad he was an experienced rower and at home on the water.

He grabbed the guitar and heaved it in between the bow and the front seat. Joey lifted the bow up and launched it into the shallow clear water, little minnows darting in all directions. Holding the bow Billie stepped in and then Joey as the little punt drifted silently away from the clearing.

"You row, okay Joey? I'll sit in the back here."

"Well, I wouldn't want a girl to row me. Wait, that didn't come out right?" Joey added, a little embarrassed.

"That's okay. I knew what you meant...just being a gentleman," Billie giggled.

Joey checked the oarlocks, unfolded the oars from the gunwales, and took up his position on the middle seat facing Billie. He rowed slowly along the shoreline. Billie grabbed one of the two lifejackets/pillows that were stuffed under the seat and reclined placing a pillow under her head, her legs dangling over the side of the boat.

The sound of an approaching power boat grew louder and louder.

"Hey, I hope that guy sees us before he gets too close," said Joey, looking off to the side.

"Oh, no!" Billie groaned, as she sat back up, recognizing the boat.

"What's the matter?" Joey asked in wonder.

"That's Paul Sinclair. He's up to his old tricks again! That's his wake boat."

As the boat loomed closer, they noticed it was pulling a slalom skier in a wet suit. The boat kept coming closer until it barely had enough space to avoid them. It suddenly swerved away. The all-too-familiar face of the skier was Paul Sinclair's. He cut out widely behind the ski boat coming toward the rowboat and then at the last second, he leaned the other way and cut back toward the boat's wake drenching Billie and Joey with a wall of water as he skied off. Completely soaked, Billie and Joey grabbed tightly to the gunwales for support as the rowboat rocked violently in the wake of the large power boat.

"That stupid jerk!" Billie shrieked.

That was absolute music to Joey's ears. He forgot how wet he was. That was wonderful to hear!

"I'll row in closer to shore where he can't get to us with the ski boat. Are you okay?" Joey asked.

"Yeah, boy, what a complete fool!" she fumed.

Joey felt like cheering her on and shouting, "More, more!" instead he just smiled to himself and headed the boat into more sheltered waters.

They found a sheltered little cove where a giant willow hung out over the water. It looked almost the same as the one at the trout hole and brought a strange familiarity to this place. Joey got the bow line and tied it to one of the branches. What little current there was, drifted them out into the warming sun. The water was only a couple feet deep here and no outboard motor would be able to navigate it.

"Hopefully, the sun will dry us out in a while. You wanna go back in and change or somethin'?" Joey asked, concerned.

"No, it's okay…Joey your guitar!"

Joey jerked around to have a look. The bottom of the case was sitting in about an inch of water. Quickly he reached over and opened the case. Luckily it was just a little damp. He took it out and set it on top of the case in the front seat to dry.

"Oh, it's okay. Just a little damp," he reassured her.

"That's good…Joe? She lay back on her side facing Joey grinning. "Can you play your guitar a little for me?… Please?"

"Well, all I can play is a few chords…nothin' fancy. It was Mom's idea to bring it along."

"So, it's here, which means you must have agreed with her and I think that is sweet that she would say that."

"Just let me hear it a bit, okay?"

How could he resist? "Alright maybe just a little," he agreed, as if his arm were being twisted off.

He cradled the guitar in his soggy lap and looked at her. Suddenly a little scowl crept onto his face. It had brought back memories of playing for Jess on the night his father had gone ballistic.

"What's wrong?" Billie wondered.

"Oh, nothin'."

"C'mon then, show me your stuff!"

"Okay, okay!" he said pretending to be irritated all the while smiling. "But first I want to ask you something."

"Sure, whaaaaat?" she droned in a silly, playful voice.

"What is it between you and Sinclair, anyway? I mean, I know it's probably none of my business, but I don't want to interfere with anything between you two, you know?"

Billie's bright, cheerful smile slowly disappeared. She dropped her head and stared down at the water. Pensive, she sat up with her hands on her knees, tilted her head with a warm understanding smile. Joey felt like he might melt.

"You have a right to know. You are just as wet as I am!" They both laughed together at their unique situation.

"He doesn't mean anything to me, believe me! His dad got me a job waiting on tables at the lodge last year. My parents and his would probably like us to get together sometime, but that's not going to happen. My dad and his dad are sort of friends. I went to a dance on a Saturday out there and I guess I kind of liked him then. I did dance with him a lot that night. It was over there at the picnic shelter by the docks of the lodge."

She pointed to the far shore and the reddish log buildings of the lodge and its boat houses.

"Oh," Joey grunted.

"But there were parents there and it really wasn't anything special. Ever since, he's been showing off and braggin' about me bein' his girl and all the rest of it. Honestly, I really think he is a jerk. I don't even like him at all anymore."

"Oh!" Joey said, a little more elevated. "I just wondered you know," Joey continued awkwardly.

"Okay then. So now you know. So, play that stupid guitar, will you?"

They both laughed again and with his anxiety quelled, Joey felt about as good as he possibly could.

Joey played a few chords and even sang "Kumbaya" and "Row Your Boat Ashore", which they thought was perfectly appropriate for today. Billie sang along with him and watched his fingers intently, always saying something nice after each little ditty. Every time Joey would look up, she acknowledged him with a responsive, reassuring smile. That twinkle in those azure eyes were electric! He felt like he was playing for a hundred thousand people in the biggest stadium in the world! Joey felt valuable, important, and strangely, not nervous. He never realized in a million years that someone he barely knew a few hours ago, could be so easy to be around.

"Joey, that's so great that you have that talent! It says a lot about someone, you know?"

After a while, they both laid back on their seats to feel the sun soaking into their faces. They took turns pointing out all the animals and faces they saw in the puffy, white clouds sliding by overhead. Joey thought about how at that moment he felt like the clouds; light, feathery and free.

Later again back on the shore, shoes back on, they turned to face each other.

"Joey?" Billie looked up smiling warmly.

"Yeah?" Joey answered, leaning on his guitar case.

"I had a great time today!... In spite of that little interruption." She said shaking her head.

"Yeah, me too. Thanks for the use of your boat."

"That's okay. Seems like you did all the work anyway. Thanks for playing for me too. We used to sing Kumbaya at camp all the time. Some people think that song is corny or something but for me it was really nice!"

Joey had the biggest urge to just grab her and hug her! No one, not Gramps, not his Mom not anyone ever, made him feel quite this way. It was a magical day and he wanted it to last forever!

"No sweat. Maybe we could do this again sometime? Joey suggested.

"I would really like that!" Billie added quickly.

"Hey, Billie, I ... I would like to show you a special place next weekend if it's alright with you. It'll have to be Sunday, though. I think I'm doomed to take piano lessons on Saturday. Would that be okay?"

"Sounds kinda mysterious! Yeah sure!"

"Well," Joey bent down to grab the handle of his guitar case. "I guess I should get going." Billie leaned in and gave him a little kiss on the cheek before he could stand up straight.

"Oh...thanks!" said Joey, slightly flushed.

"Yeah, I gotta go too. See ya," Billie turned and walked toward home through the brush.

"See, ya."

Joey was euphoric! He couldn't have imagined a better day! He turned to float home and as he walked, he was in another dimension. He didn't hear the birds, the squirrels chattering, the traffic on the road or the jackhammer tearing up the sidewalk across the street. He didn't smell the pines, feel the sun or the gentle warm breeze. He just found himself walking up his laneway.

Then a thought occurred to him, "Thanks!... I said thanks. Are you kidding? Thanks? Billie kissed me and I said thanks? What a dork!"

Joey half laughed to himself and figured he needed to work on his relationship finesse, but she kissed him and that is all that mattered to him!

CHAPTER NINE

It was a cool, misty morning as Joey waited on the side of the road and watched Jug emerge from the front door of his green clapboard, frame house. Jug's family wasn't much better off financially than Joey's. His Father had passed away a few years ago and his mom worked at a Walmart in the city. Jug's dad used to work in the city too but had never taken out any life insurance so what little they had was hard to come by.

They walked along towards school talking about nothing in particular for quite some time. Joey was in a better mood then he had been in weeks. He felt, somehow, stronger, more alive, more awake, and happier to be who he was. He tried to hold back his enthusiasm even though he wanted the whole world to know that Billie thought he was, "Okay" despite what everybody else thought!... but Jug noticed.

"So, man, how'd it go with Billie on the weekend? Jug finally offered. "By the way you seem to be feeling, I'd say you musta' done alright."

"Yeah, things went pretty good, I guess." Joey wanted to remain a little mysterious just to keep Jug hungry enough to keep digging.

"Not to be nosy but, what did you guys do? Did she let you kiss her?" Jug prodded, smacking Joey on the shoulder.

Joey mused about how Jug could be a real moron sometimes. To him, making out with a girl was the only way to tell if there was something going on. That probably explained why he never really had any girls as friends.

"None of your business, buddy." Joey continued trying to keep his pride intact. "I know she likes me though and we had a good time. We went out on the lake in her rowboat."

"OOO, sounds romantic!" he teased with a giant grin.

"Well, as a matter of fact, it kinda was," Joey admitted.

"How are you gonna deal with Mr. Sinclair when he finds out?"

Joey recalled how Sinclair had seen them out there and felt clouds forming over his head.

"He already knows. He buzzed us with his boat and saw us. Billie said she didn't like him anymore...He can go to hell!"

"Sounds brave, Joe, but you know Sinclair. He's a dick and probably a pretty sore loser. I think you better watch out for him."

"Yeah, I know. It's a good thing he lives halfway around the lake and rides the school bus. I can usually avoid him in the mornings."

"Just be careful, that's all. I won't tell anybody that she likes you but I'm sure he will put 2 and 2 together sooner or later."

"Yeah, yeah, I know," Joey shrugged coolly.

Joey was glad he had told Jug about the boat incident. It felt as though he had someone else, besides Billie on his side and it provided a little inner strength.

He did avoid Sinclair for most of the morning. He saw Billie briefly a couple of times in the hallways, just to smile and say hey. Once, she was walking by with a bunch of other girls, gabbing up a storm. Even as part of the gaggle she managed to look Joey's way, tilt her head, make a silly face and wave. Her eyes snagged him again! He was sure she would not have done that a week ago.

Grabbing his lunch out of his locker he turned to head down to the cafeteria when he felt a painful jab on his shoulder and was being pushed backwards up against the lockers landing with a metallic thud. Knees bent, he stood staring up the nostrils of Paul Sinclair pinning him to the wall of lockers. Joey didn't know what to say.

"What are you doin?" Joey finally emitted weakly.

"Look, Joe-boy, I know you're tryin' to move in on Billie and I don't like it!... Comprendez?"

Sinclair grabbed the neck of Joey's shirt and poked his finger viciously into his chest.

"We were just out for a little ride!" Joey answered shakily. Then feeling some new strength returning. "Let go of my shirt!"

Joey wriggled free as Sinclair loosened his hold somewhat. They stood glaring at each other. The people passing in the hall were just a blur to Joey but he could feel them rubbernecking as they walked by. He stifled the ridiculous notion that he might start to cry but his emotions were so intense! He wanted to duck or run or do whatever it took to survive.

"Yeah, I saw you, remember?" Sinclair started again, just as hotly. "I am giving you a warning. Stay away from her or you'll be damn sorry!"

Sinclair grabbed Joey's lunch out of his hand, threw it to the floor and stomped on it reducing the contents to mush. His eyes never left Joey's as he fed on his obvious terror.

"I'm not going to knock the crap out of you here. I can't risk losing my year over a little asshole like you! I'm telling you, if you don't back off there will be nothing to hold me back once we're off the school grounds!"

He turned and walked away down the hall.

Joey spent his lunch period outside on the bench by the traffic circle. He wasn't particularly hungry now anyway. He knew there had to be something he could do but he didn't know what that could be. All he knew for sure was that he wanted the feeling he had on Saturday. To deal with Sinclair he needed the confidence that Billie had brought out in him. His mind wandered back to the lake, the rowboat, and Billie. His lack of courage caused him to be confused. What messages did she intend him to receive? She held his hand. Well, she had actually just pulled him over to see her boat. She said she enjoyed the guitar playing. Was she just trying to be nice? There was the kiss. Was that just something girls did when they had a good time…just a thank you? Joey tried to recall all the little things they did and said. In his fragile state he could not actually decide whether she really liked him or was just having fun kicking around with someone for the afternoon.

Then he remembered something. She had said, "Joey, I had a great time today." It was a small thing but to Joey very significant. It wasn't that he had been partly responsible for her having a good time. It was that she had called him, "Joey!" He realized that little change from, "Joe" was endearing and was responsible, in part, for making him warmer and feeling closer to her. He noticed it at the time but only now did it sink in. How did she know she could get away with calling him that? The only people that called him that, other than Jess when she was in a sucky mood, or Pam when she wanted something, were his mom and Gramps.

Joey felt a longing to see her and talk to her. What was this? There had never been anyone that he felt this way about. Joey just couldn't get his head around this emotional consciousness and the pressure growing in his chest. The buzzer marking the end of the lunch period was about to ring. He ran back into the school hoping to catch her by her locker between classes. As he bounded up the stairs and burst through the doors on the second floor the buzzer sounded. Down the hallway he continued briskly. He was in luck! Rounding the corner, he caught her as she worked away on her lock. Joey was a little out of breath but just the sight of her made him feel better.

Catching his breath and trying to look casual he uttered, "Hey, Billie."

"Hey, Joe," she answered cheerfully, turned and leaned on her locker facing him, a few books clutched to her chest.

"Look, I know we don't have much time to talk right now, and this is kinda short notice, but...Do you wanna walk over to my house after school today? Mom and Jess won't be around. Maybe we could watch a DVD or play x-box or just talk, whatever?"

Joey was afraid that his desperation might be showing through.

"Sure, I guess so," Billie answered.

"Great, gotta go...see ya later."

Joey ran off, pretending to be late for a class.

After school, Billie, Jug and Joey were walking up the narrow backroad toward Joey's house. Joey felt that he must have been frantic to invite Billie to his lowly home. He hoped she would not feel like his house was too meager or even creepy. It seemed that he had to be with her somewhere that was not public, as Sinclair's threats were still ringing in his ears.

They dropped Jug off and as they neared Joey's laneway, Harriet was running back and forth wagging her tail in anticipation.

"Wow, is that your dog?" Billie asked enthusiastically.

"Yeah, that's Harriet. She loves people!"

"Geez, she's beautiful! She seems so happy to see you!"

"Yeah, we're kinda buddies," Joey answered. "Most days, she is my best friend. We do a lot of things together back in the bush and along the shore here. Looks like she's happy to see you too!"

"Aw, hi Harriet!" Billie let out, in a baby voice. "What a good girl you are!"

Billie got down on her knees and Harriet was all over her almost wagging her tail off and licking her to death. Harriet smiled so hard she sneezed and reached her paw out knocking Billie over into the pine needles. They rolled on the ground laughing and both were immediate friends."

"Boy, does she ever like you!" Joey remarked.

"I've never seen a nicer dog. I love her!" Billie spitted out, while getting her face washed by Harriet's flailing tongue.

"How did you train her to stay on your property so nice?" Billie wondered.

"When she was a pup, Mom and Dad had one of those invisible fences. It gave her a little shock when she got too close to the edge of the property. Pam and I didn't like that, so we made them take it off her. She would yelp when she got shocked, and we didn't want to hurt her. She has never forgotten that feeling and won't go off the yard unless I'm leading her. Even then, she hesitates until I convince her that it's okay. Maybe it was a good thing. I don't know. At least we are fairly sure she won't run out and get hit by a car."

"Well, that's good, because she's amazing!" Billie continued still dancing around and playing.

Eventually, they found themselves facing each other at the kitchen table. Joey was more than a little embarrassed by the old cottage he called home, but Billie looked quite comfortable and only said nice things about it. She mentioned how pretty the trees were around the lot and that she really liked the curtains on the kitchen window that his mom had made. He offered her a coke and they sat there sipping and talking. Some of the doubts and insecurities Joey had felt earlier in the day were gradually fading.

Billie spotted something on the shelf on the side of the cupboards by the window and she went over and picked it up. It was one of Joey's family's little book-sized photo albums.

"Do you mind if I look at this?" she asked.

"Yeah sure. I mean, no I don't mind," he answered. He realized there were naked baby pictures of him in there but, what the heck!

She flipped through the pages and Joey noticed the expressions on her face changing with each photo she spotted. She laughed and covered her mouth with one hand as she pointed with the other hand to a picture labeled, "Joey in tub-eight months". Joey smiled shyly. He was confused that she would be that interested in him, or that his family pictures would attract her in the least.

"You sure have a lot of photos in here with your Grandad," she offered finally.

"Yeah, I suppose so. We used to do a lot of things together."

"Is he still alive?" Billie looked up.

"Yeah, he lives over at the William's Glen Senior Residence. I guess we don't do quite as much anymore because he is slowin' down a bit. I still go over and see him all the time."

Joey thought more about how Gramps was during his last visit and how he seemed to have watery eyes every time Joey was about to leave. The recollection made his demeanor sadden slightly.

"You are really close to your grandad, aren't you, Joey? She looked up at Joey knowingly, nodding.

"yeah, I guess I am," Joey agreed, watching her eyes twinkle with understanding. "You know, other than Mom and Gramps, you are the only one that has ever called me Joey."

Joey could not believe he had just let that out. He prayed that she wouldn't think that he was trying to come on to her or something. Perhaps he was fishing again for her true feelings about him.

"Oh, that's really sweet!" Billie said with a big smile on her face.

"What about you? Do you have a favorite grandparent?" Joey asked.

"No, I don't have any anymore."

"Oh, sorry, I didn't know."

"That's Okay," replied Billie. "Grandparents are special. I used to be close to my Nanny Jo. Her real name was Josephine but for a little girl Jo was a whole lot easier to say, so I just knew her as Nanny Jo."

"That's cool, and you're right, grandparents are special. It's hard for me to imagine life without Gramps!" It was hard for Joey to say that and Billie sensed it.

"What about your dad? Where does he work?" Billie asked innocently, trying to be more upbeat.

That question was like an arrow in his chest, and he tried his best to avoid answering it directly as it took him by surprise. "He works at the grist mill in Montrose and he's away for a while." He couldn't hide his feelings completely, and Billie noticed a tinge of pain impair his mood.

Billie reached across the table with both her hands and held Joey's in a comforting gesture.

After a little while Joey walked Billie back to her place. About a block away, just before the park beside her house, Billie reached out for Joey to take her hand. Joey gave her hand a playful squeeze and hung on. Hand in hand they cut through the park and the willowy bushes along the shore on a small path that led past the little rowboat and eventually to an open area of grass in the backyard of Billie's house. The big difference for Joey was that this time they were holding hands and she was not just leading him somewhere.

As soon as they got to the open area on Billie's back lawn she turned, faced him and reached out her other hand. Joey took it in his other hand and was completely riveted by those amazing blue eyes!

"Joey, I really like you!" she said sincerely.

"I really like you too, Billie!"

She stretched up on her tiptoes and gave Joey a kiss on the cheek then turned and ran off toward her house.

Joey once again walked home, his chest pounding, unaffected by his other physical senses, and already wondering when he could see her again.

CHAPTER TEN

That kiss answered all his questions, he thought, as he walked up the gravel road toward his house. Billie's sweet lips still burning on his cheek, he felt like he might never wash his face again! Suddenly, he could hear birds chirping, cicadas drilling out their shrill mating calls and the whirring of the wind in the pines overhead awakening that wonderful smell that Joey loved. Instead of a numbing inflection, he experienced after other meetings with Billie he seemed to have a heightened sense of appreciation of everything around him, at least for the time being. The whole world seemed better somehow. At a sunny patch on the side of the road he looked up at the sky drinking in the warmth hoping no one was watching as he grinned like an idiot. He took a deep breath and felt icy little prickles of sheer happiness running up his spine. This dreamy state, however, was not to last.

Joey stood frozen in his tracks after rounding the last bend and spotting a police car in his driveway! Despite fearing what he might find when he got there, he picked up his pace and began to run. As he burst into the kitchen, he found his mom and a police officer sitting at the table where Billie and he had been not more than half an hour ago. They both looked up quickly at Joey's abrupt entry. His mom had been crying but she blinked quickly trying to force a smile, but the smeared eye shadow betrayed her effort.

"Joseph, this is Constable Richards," she said in her most dignified voice.

"Hello, young man."

He stood up extending a huge hand. Joey just stood there looking from one to the other, not able to say anything as he shook the hulking cop's hand.

"Come over here and sit down," Lilley said, while pushing out a chair with her foot.

"What's the matter, Mom? Joey asked, agitated, and nauseated by the look on his mom's face.

"Calm down, Joey. I will explain things to you in a minute."

She looked over at the cop and then back to Joey.

Sensing that she needed time with Joey, Constable Richards stood up and pushed the chair in to the table holding his hat in his hand.

"Well, I gotta be getting' back to the station. I'll see my way out. Sorry this couldn't have been a more pleasant meeting, Mrs. Burgess. I'll see you tomorrow then. Good day, Joseph."

"He opened the door with one hand and adjusted his hat with the other and ducked through the doorway."

"Mom, what's goin' on?" Jocy pleaded.

"Easy honey, just let me explain."

Joey didn't like the sound of this already. She hardly ever called him honey, and she looked so tired and sad. As she attempted to gather herself Joey started to panic. Even Harriet was standing looking up at Lilley with her head on a slight tilt wondering what was happening.

"Is it Dad?...Is it Gramps?...Is something wrong with Gramps?" Joey begged as tears began to form in his eyes.

"Joseph! Stop, please! It's not your dad or your grandfather. Just try to be quiet and listen!"

Joey tried to calm himself and testily wiped the stupid tear away before it started sliding down his cheek. That made him think briefly of how Billie kissed him there and a mild surge of strength engulfed him.

"Mom, just tell me!"

"Okay, but don't interrupt. Just let me tell you before you ask anything...It's Pamela. She's in very serious trouble. The police raided a cottage over on Lakeshore Drive and found Pam and Tom, her boyfriend, and several other people doing drugs. It wasn't just alcohol or marijuana, it was cocaine. They were snorting cocaine up their noses! They even found some other drugs too. I don't even remember all the names!"

With that she held her head in her hands and began to cry. Joey remembered his dad making her cry like that. He knew she wanted to say more so he put his head down and waited as anger welled up inside him. He couldn't stand to see her this way! He started thinking of who was to blame for this and instantly thought of his dad. If he only had a good loving father, someone who would be there for his mom and his sisters, this family wouldn't be so messed up!

Lilley began again, taking deep breaths to regain her composure. "She's not going to be home for a while. The police are holding her for questions and whatever else they have to do while they investigate where the drugs came from and all that," she shrugged in frustration. "I just can't afford bail money, so I guess she might as well stay there for now. They gotta find out who's selling that stuff to these kids. I don't know…I…I just didn't know!"

She folded her arms and buried her face in them crying again. Joey walked around behind her and hugged her laying his head on her shoulder. He wanted desperately to make things better. How could he give her what she had given him on the night his dad had gone so crazy? His tears were landing on her arm. She stood up slowly, turned around and lifted Joey's head with her hand under his chin.

"I love you, Joey! Don't ever forget that!"

"I know, Mom…me too."

She hugged Joey tightly. Joey felt the unconditional nature of her love which made him wonder why he had so much trouble telling the people closest to him that he loved them. He chalked it up to just being a dumb teenager.

Joey watched as his mom slipped on a hoodie and left to go pick up Jess. She was over at the Jordan's about a mile further down the road. She often did spot duty babysitting when Pam wasn't available. It looked like she was not going to be available for a little while! How was his mom going to explain this one to Jess?

That night, with Jess in bed, Lilley had settled into an easy chair in the TV room. The TV wasn't on. There was a soap opera playing out vividly in her mind. This soap was her life and her family! She stared blankly out the window feeling the anguish that a mother feels when one of her babies was being held captive. The helplessness overcame her several times as she wept off and on for an hour thinking of Pamela in a cold jail cell. She blamed herself for everything!

Joey had been in his room for a while, thinking that his mom needed some space. Besides, he didn't want to talk about it. He and Pam had many tiffs in the last year or so, but she was his sister and he felt lousy for her. He sat propped up on his bed strumming quietly thinking that musicians must use moments like this for inspiration. There came a knock on his door, and he invited his mom in. She sat down on the edge of the bed.

"Joey, are you okay?" she asked quietly.

"Yeah, I guess so," he replied. Although Joey hadn't really sorted out all his feelings yet. He had a way of diverting his attention to other things to avoid all the negative stuff. This process did not always work perfectly but sometimes it helped ease things for the moment.

"There's something else you should know," she continued. "... about your father."

"Joey interrupted, "Mom, I know that you have somehow kept him away from here. I think I kinda know how too. It's got somethin' to do with lawyers and legal stuff. I learn a few things from TV, you know. I think I can figure it out."

Lilley raised her eyebrows and nodded, "Well, I was hoping that you had. I know you're not a little boy anymore. You are right, of course. Right now, he is under legal orders to stay away from here. They call it a restraining order. We don't know how long it will take, Joey, but he obviously needs to get help. I don't know if it will take months or a year or longer." She continued pushing back the tears, "There's always the possibility that he may never come back home. Do you understand, Joey?"

"Yes, I do Mom. I've thought about that, too.

Joey realized that thinking about it was one thing, but the reality was something else. He knew that when families split up the effects are tumultuous for every family member. He understood that Jess didn't really need to know the details. With his father not around, there was a void there but lately Hank's involvement with Lilley and the kids were largely negative encounters. Joey could remember when he used to do things with his dad...things like hiking in the woods or fishing in the old rowboat. He recalled though, that there was always a six pack or a flask with his dad nearly every time. He would have not realized then, how this was a harbinger of things to come. He remembered Hank holding Jess and even falling asleep with her in the hammock out back. So, as far as Jess was concerned it was probably better to keep her from the exact truth for the time being. There had been love, maybe there still was, but Joey didn't understand how someone's father could call his son a little bastard and still love him. That doesn't even make sense. How could alcohol distort a person's behavior that badly? There was something telling Joey that his father was somehow not there when the alcohol took over his brain.

Joey wondered if Pam's latest difficulty with drugs was a direct result of the family crisis. He had heard how some teenagers would resort to overeating or engage in activities that erroneously gave them some small pleasure not realizing or caring about the long-term consequences. He guessed that Pam was escaping the situation at home through drug use and the camaraderie of her like-minded friends.

What was the hardest for Joey was that deep down inside he didn't really hate his father. It was more fear and apprehension for the future and even concern for his family's health.

He wondered if his way of escaping was being with Billie. Was he that starved for positive interaction or was it just a normal friendship, the result of mutual feelings?

He thought about his mom more than anything. His mom and dad had obviously been close, in love and had clearly vowed to take care of each other through the consecration of marriage. What had gone so terribly wrong? Was it all alcohol? Was he partially to blame? Was his mom partially to blame? He had never heard his mom say anything bad about his dad or talk to him crossly unless he was abusing her when he was drunk. Joey felt extreme compassion for his mom. He reasoned that because she had the most history with him and had pledged herself to him, that she had the most to lose. It was likely, as well, that besides the loss of her husband, she would feel guilt and responsibility for the breakup. Joey relied on the hope that the future would see his family once again whole and healthy. For now, he promised himself to support his mom where he could and try to avoid confrontations that could cause her any more grief.

It had been several minutes, both of them sitting on Joey's bed, Lilley staring out the window and Joey staring at the wall in contemplation.

Finally, Lilley offered, "I see you've got your guitar out. How did things go with Billie? Did you play it for her?" She forced a contrived cheerfulness.

"Yeah, I did. Things went pretty good. I hate to admit it, but that was a really good idea!" Joey smiled with a twinkle.

"Good, I'm glad. Friends are valuable. She's a nice girl too. The local gossipers down at the store say she is a really good babysitter and sensible, too. Well, I think I'm going to turn in… Good night, Joey," she added cuffing Joey's bare foot, playfully.

"'Night, Mom."

After she left, Joey put his guitar back in its case, laid back folding his arms under his head and tried not to let anything negative enter his thoughts. Trees, water, sun, fish, Billie, and all the ways those thoughts stimulated his senses took him away into a needed slumber.

Joey was not exactly sure how to describe what woke him up, but it was obviously early and not near time to get ready for school. Once again, he was damp with sweat. Waking this way was making him wonder why. It didn't seem hot in his bedroom. He had always been a sound sleeper. His head was buzzing like an electrical transformer. He shook his head to find out if he was really awake. It was a phenomenon that was becoming more frequent...sparks and snapping noises scaring him and causing him to bolt upright and then slouch back down against the wall.

He became aware of his consciousness and starting thinking confusing and disjointed thoughts. It was as though there were thousands of thoughts flitting around in his head all at once. He felt his chest and abdomen tighten like a rock. Attempting to reduce the tension and calm himself, he took deep breaths. He felt haunted by all the things in his life. He was bad, messed up, dumb, and poor. His father called him a bastard! He listened to that word echoing as if his dad was shouting it in a huge hall. Everything was wrong and nothing was right and now his sister was a druggie! All the worst parts of his life gripped him as if they were giant fingers wrapping around his body and squeezing so hard that he could barely breathe!

Joey perceived that this awful tension and strain went on for what seemed like hours. It was as though he was in a daze and too tense and paralyzed to get up and do anything. He wanted to flick off the evil switch or jump in a hole to hide from everything and just wait there until his universe was good and peaceful again.

Lilley called for him to get up. He opened his eyes and couldn't determine if the night he had just experienced was a dream or he had been awake for most of it. He suspected he was at least partially awake since he was still sweaty and tired, like you might feel after taking part in a vigorous contact sport. He got up and went through all his morning routines but felt strangely numb. If a bolt of lightning struck the ground beside him, he would not have flinched.

As he walked down the gravel road toward Jug's house, he knew it was a sunny day. He was mildly cognizant of birds chirping. He was dimly aware of everything he liked about this environment but there was something cold and black gripping his heart.

CHAPTER ELEVEN

Joey could not recall ever starting a day in a fouler mood. Between being overtired and his preoccupation with his lot in life, everything seemed rather pointless. Everyone in the town of William's Glen was well aware of the big drug raid and likely knew who all the participants were as well. It was hard to keep anything secret in a small town like this. In fact, that was probably the biggest news to ever hit town since Sally McDonald won the district public speaking contest last year! Nothing of real consequence ever seemed to happen here.

Obviously, Jug knew all about the situation because there was a tension between the two this morning. Joey was drained from lack of sleep and didn't want to talk about it anyway and Jug was afraid to mention anything that might upset Joey. As close friends, they knew when the other was about to snap with only the slightest provocation.

Joey sat preoccupied and stewing through all of his classes. He didn't see Billie anywhere, and he was almost glad. He didn't want her to see him suffering this misery and he felt like nothing could make him feel happy or enthusiastic about his present life.

At lunch Jug and Joey sat in the cafeteria; Joey eating his sandwich and Jug slurping up noodles from his spaghetti. Joey remembered seeing back in the kitchen a few months ago and vowed not to order anything that came from there. Besides, he loved his favorite sandwiches...peanut butter, bologna, sweet pickles and ketchup. Whenever he told people what he was eating they would usually gag, but it was something that his dad used to make, and he grew to like them too. Thoughts of his dad made him slightly gloomier again.

Jug was going on about chemistry class, and how he didn't understand how solid things could have little electrons buzzing around inside them like Mr. Vanderloop so graphically illustrated in class. Joey, half listening, just nodded his head at the right times and resigned to accept Jug's chatter as part of the background noises of the room. Still in somber reflection he took the occasional half-hearted bite out of his sandwich while questioning his reason for being.

As Joey crumbled up his sandwich wrap and shifted in his seat to get ready to go outside for a while, a paper missile hit him in the left temple and splatted its cargo of ketchup all over his shirt and down one side of his pants! Startled he jerked his chair back from the table. Looking down at himself and up to find where it came from, the cafeteria erupted with a variety of reactions. There was squealing, some groaning with empathy at the mess but mostly wild frenzied laughter. The scraping of chair legs could be heard as almost everyone stood to get a better view. Many continued laughing and some of the girls were holding their hands over their mouths shocked by the sight. Joey found the wadded paper towel in his lap and flung it on the table. Jug passed him a napkin and he wiped his face of red ketchup speckles and dabbed his shirt. At the same time Joey was burning up inside. He knew the direction the ketchup bomb came from and he knew who was responsible. The snickers and cackles continued as he felt so out of control and flustered. He was like a fallen gladiator with the enemy's sword at his throat, as a crowd of blood-thirsty spectators gave the thumbs down calling for his demise. He felt anger, fear and extreme embarrassment all at the same time! He could not see or focus on anything. He rose to his feet, trembling, unsure of where to flee. The crowd in the room was undiscernible like a blurred swarm of flies. Joey summoned some courage and smiled in an attempt to reduce the perpetrator's satisfaction and save some fragment of dignity. Then he lowered his head and gritted his teeth unsure of where to lash out first.

From across the room, he heard his voice, "Hey, Joe-boy, cut yourself shavin' this mornin?"

Joey looked up in the direction of the voice and he could make out Sinclair with his bunch of puppets howling, pounding their table, kicking their feet and almost crying in ultimate satisfaction.

Joey wanted to kill him! There was no room for the voice of reason. He sincerely wanted to end him! He noticed Jug's bread knife and clenched it in his right hand instinctively, as some of the students nearby gasped. As he raged inside, he felt Jug grab his arm and pin it to the table with surprising strength.

"Don't be stupid Joe!" he pleaded. "Sit down!...Sit down!... For God's sake!" Jug's voice was desperate and cracking.

Joey fell back down into his seat, releasing the knife into Jug's custody. He was shaking and terrified by his own thoughts! He placed his elbows on the table and held his head between his hands looking downward. What was once general hysteria throughout the cafeteria began to calm with the understanding that the show was about over.

Joey looked up to Jug's frantic whisper, "Man, Joe, you seriously almost lost it!" Then with relief added, "Get him some other way…some other time. You need to cool off. He wants you to confront him so that he can show everyone how big he is. Besides, you didn't really see him throw it so he can just plead innocence."

"That son-of-a-bitch!" Joey growled, infuriated.

Joey could feel another surge of anger beginning to erupt. Those stupid tears began to well in his eyes! He had no escape and no matter how he reacted now, the humiliation had already occurred. He stood up and ran out of the cafeteria and down the hall as Sinclair's elated laughter faded behind him. Joey didn't stop running until he was a block away from school. Away from the scene and the sounds, he slowed down, hands on his knees breathing deeply and feeling nauseous. Bending over he wretched slightly and began to think a little more clearly, he realized there was no way he could go back there. He would tell the office on Monday that he got sick and went home.

Joey sat down on an old stump on the side of the road to catch his breath and take stock of what just happened. Negativity engulfed him with self-deprecation, wondering how he had become the butt of Sinclair's sadism and why so many sided with him. Besides Jug, no one else had come to his rescue. As the clouds gave way to a warm shaft of sunshine, he envisioned his appearance sitting there on the side of the road. Not only did he reek of ketchup emphasized by the sun, but it could only be interpreted as an accident victim covered in blood! He allowed himself a weak, delirious chuckle.

He picked himself up and turned into Gramps' place just to get off the street. He spotted him on the picnic bench having his lunch. Still smoldering and rattled, Joey plunked himself across from him on the seat.

"Good lord, Joey...Are you hurt?"

"It's just ketchup." Joey snarled back.

"Aren't you supposed to be at school?"

Joey thought visiting Gramps right now might not have been a great idea. Still seething, he knew he didn't have the patience to be civil.

"I gotta go home and clean up." Joey offered.

Gramps studied Joey's bizarre appearance with the red stains all over the front and side of him and ketchup crusting on his neck.

Trying to add some levity to the situation, Gramps let out a wheezing chortle, "You know, Joey, you look like something out of a horror movie. Is this Friday the thirteenth?" He laughed more heartily now letting out a snort as he caught his breath.

This from Gramps? Joey was shocked. There was nothing remotely funny about what happened to him today. At least it was too soon to reflect on it that way.

"Why don't you just get a real good laugh? You stupid old fart!"

Ripping his shirt off and throwing it to the ground, Joey wheeled around and ran for the cover of the bush behind the tool shed. He found himself in the sanctity, and comfort of his favorite place in the world. Joey sat with his bare back up against the smooth grey bark of the giant beech tree. He dropped his head between his knees and wept, his anxious thoughts whirring around inside him. Would he ever be able to face things? Would he ever stop reacting like a baby? He wiped off the tears with the back of his hand and flung them to the ground like they were something gross. Why was he such a lousy person? He kept seeing the hurt look in Gramps' old eyes after he had taken out the whole day and night on him. It was an endless circle...the self-pity, as he tried to reason why he had drawn this lot in life, then the feeling of guilt for thinking of himself so much and how he had reacted today. Was he a mass murderer in his previous life? Is karma being administered? He wanted a way out. He thought about tying a boulder to his ankles and jumping off the town bridge. Instead, he buried his face in his arms and sobbed again, feeling completely confused and effectively destroyed!

After an hour had passed, Joey finally looked up and experienced a subtle shift in emotion. He began to feel his mood surrender to the calming influence of this place. He thought of how he was fortunate to have such a hideout. The mammoth American beech tree overlooking the bubbling water was his refuge; a place only he knew about. It really was a beautiful. If he laid down in the soft grass and leaves no one could see him there because it was on a mound and no one usually looked up there. The small saplings and bushes surrounding the clearing where he sat were now in full leaf which provided more cover. He needed this place more than he ever had before.

Joey thought once more about his current state. He was now topless with red marks around his neck, chest and arms, stains on his jeans and completely disheveled hair. He imagined himself running out of the bush like he was a werewolf just returning to his human form. He had viciously attacked and devoured some other animal or maybe even human! Thinking of this image, he could not help but to laugh right out loud!

That evening, after explaining to his mom about how the lid of the ketchup flew off when he shook it, he retired to bed early. He halfheartedly strummed a few chords on his guitar before attempting sleep. Joey found that the minor chords appealed to his melancholy mood and how when you string just minor chords together, you could make up a somber melody. It brought to mind his guilt for how horribly he had treated Gramps. Beginning to fade he barely made out the sound of the phone ringing in the kitchen.

Shortly after, Lilley tapped lightly on his door and said softly, "The phone's for you, Joe."

Joey was hoping it wasn't Gramps. He didn't know how he was going to talk to him after his outburst.

"Is it Gramps?" Joey asked.

"Ah, nope," Lilley answered in an odd tone.

Joey got up and took a seat at the kitchen table and held the phone gingerly to his ear, "Hello?"

"Hi, Joey? It's Billie."

"Oh, hi, Billie," Joey answered with a slight exhale of relief.

Hearing that voice was like a soothing medicine.

"I had to go into the city this morning with Mom. I noticed you weren't at school this afternoon. Are you sick or something?" she asked with genuine concern.

"Uh, no. I just didn't feel too good after lunch, so I came home to rest. I'm okay now, though."

It wasn't a lie.

"Do you have those piano lessons tomorrow?" she asked.

"No, Mom's still busy in the city. Why?"

"Do you think we could get together tomorrow instead of Sunday? My parents are having my aunt and uncle over on Sunday and they would kinda like me to be around." Billie dragged the sentence out slowly as if she was disappointed and sorry to let Joey down.

"Um, yeah, sure. How about meetin' down at the bridge, like, around ten?" Joey suggested.

"Sounds great. I'll bring lunch." She answered cheerfully.

"Awesome! I'll see ya then,"

"Okay...bye."

"Bye."

Joey hung up quietly, glanced over and noticed his mom who was darning some socks at the other end of the table. He knew that she had overheard everything.

Hoping she wouldn't say anything, he slipped gingerly past her issuing a, "'Night, mom."

"'Night Joe." Lilly answered, without another word.

Joey lay awake for several minutes thinking about Billie. He wondered about her existence in his life and felt strangely lucky. This was a rare thought for him. Sometimes sitting on the rocks in the back bay with Harriet at his feet and fishing pole in hand, he had similar feelings. The environment in which he lived could bestow pangs of joy or at least contentment for short periods of time. He thought how being happy doesn't have to mean everything is going perfectly. Joey wondered if the world would be so different if he had lots of money or if he had a perfect, happy family. He remembered his mom's words after she had purchased a meagre birthday present, wrapped it in brown packaging paper and presented it to him after school last April. He looked at the parcel, shook it, and examined it with a puzzled look trying to guess its contents.

"It's not much Joey. It doesn't matter what it's wrapped in or even what it is, as long as it is given with love!"

Her gift was a beautiful bone-handled filet knife and two spinner lures. Joey knew how much this type of tackle cost and how his mom would have had to do some fancy saving in order to provide him with such a gift.

Joey thought the metaphor of the wrapping paper and the gift was somehow sent to Joey as the answer to his question. The thought of being in some parallel universe where he was rich and had an ideal family was becoming slightly less important. It was merely wrapping paper and if it had been fancy wrapping paper it would not have changed what was inside. He actually had something that Paul Sinclair didn't have, and that brought a slight smile as he drifted off to sleep.

CHAPTER TWELVE

On his way out the door the next morning, Lilley handed Joey two dollars.

"Thanks, Mom. What's that for?"

Lilley smiled, "Pick up a couple pops at the store. You shouldn't go empty-handed on a date...I mean, you shouldn't go empty-handed to meet a friend," she said grinning behind a cupped hand.

Joey was aware of the teasing nature in which she presented the money, but he also realized that it was a good idea. It was like his mom was encouraging this relationship and just wanted him to be happy.

Joey found Harriet sprawled out in the still shaded porch. She perked up wagging her tale in anticipation of an outing at the lake. Joey felt a little guilty patting her head and telling her to stay, but three was a crowd today! Hot, muggy air like you might expect near the end of July hit Joey as soon as he stepped into the sunshine and he was glad that he wore his shorts and muscle shirt. Not only would the breeze have maximum effect, but he could show her that he wasn't just skin and bones. He grabbed a couple of cokes at the store and spotted Billie in the distance standing peering over the rail of the bridge. She was mesmerized by the swiftly flowing current as it bubbled over the stony creek bottom. She had a cooler resting beside her and an old quilt folded up between the handles. As he approached her, she smiled warmly. They exchanged, "HI's" and she took the cokes from Joey and slipped them into her cooler.

In just those few seconds when their eyes met, Joey concluded that every time he saw her, she looked prettier. It was as if the more he got to know her, the more attractive she looked to him. It was something he had never thought of before. A person's smile, the sound of their voice, the way they treat you and the quality of their character, can actually make them appear better looking.

Joey reached down and grabbed the cooler handles while Billie snatched up the quilt.

"C'mon, I want to show you something!" Joey said enthusiastically.

They crossed the road, found the path alongside the stream and headed south towards the trout hole. At first the path was narrow, weaving around huge boulders near lake and the mouth of the stream and gradually it disappeared with no discernable trail the further they walked. They continued single file, with Joey being the tour guide, catching branches so they wouldn't spring back into Billie's face. In a clearing where they could walk side by side Joey reached out his empty hand and Billie took it with a smile. They both felt excited, recognizing the bond that they were forming and holding hands was like the real, non-metaphorical attachment.

"What a difference a day makes!" thought joey.

To Joey's utter surprise and amazement, Billie pulled Joey to a stop, reached up on tippy-toes and kissed him on the lips! Then she stood back looking into his eyes smiling affectionately.

"Wow!" Joey remarked, stunned. "What was that for?"

"I wanted to tell you that I am happy to be with you and I thought that was the best way."

"Message received, loud and clear! Anytime you feel happy you know where to find me!" Then pausing and adding with emphasis, "You have no idea how happy you make me!"

They gave each other a big one-armed hug. They were the only people on earth, and this was their personal Garden of Eden!

They continued through the long grass and bushes winding their way along the bank of the stream. At the trout hole Joey set down the cooler and ran around to the hollow of the big willow and returned with his fishing pole and tackle box he had stashed there. They stood side-by-side on a flat rock while Joey made a few casts downstream into the eddy of the pooling water just ahead of some more turbulent whitewater. On his third cast he caught a little speckled trout while Billie reacted in excited laughter. Joey thought it was as though she'd never seen a fish before. Jokingly, Joey held up the squirming little mini trout and asked her to take it off the hook. Billie just turned up her nose and suggested that he could do the honors. Once freed, they both remarked on the coloring of the little beast and Joey vowed that someday that would be dinner.

"Hey, Joey...can I try?" Billie asked excitedly.

Joey showed her how to cast and explained how to run the bail on the spinning reel as simply as he could with a few slow-motion examples. She obviously hadn't done this kind of thing before which Joey thought was strange since she lived right on the lake. Nevertheless, she proved to be a quick learner and on her second try made a remarkably accurate cast. Joey remembered the time he caught Gramps' hat and ripped it right off his head when he was first learning. They both stood there laughing away as Joey shared that story with her.

Suddenly, she squealed," I got one! I got one!"

"Keep the line tight! Don't let him swim toward you and make it go slack!"

She fidgeted awkwardly with the reel at first but gradually was making headway. She laughed and giggled with intermittent shrieks of both thrill and what seemed like terror!

Joey could tell by the bow in the pole that it was actually a good fish – a pan fry sized speckle. It thrashed about wildly splashing them both as she reeled it in closer to the rocky shore.

"What do I do? What do I do? Billie pleaded. "Joey, get it! Get it!"

Joey reached over and calmly took the line, steadied it and grabbed the now exhausted trout by the gills. Thankfully, it was barely hooked through the fish's cartilaginous lip, so he unhooked it carefully and brought it over to show her.

"Eww, you grabbed it right by its mouth?" She questioned. "Doesn't that hurt? Won't it bite you?" she added, still animated.

"That's okay," Joey answered. "They don't have much for teeth." He showed her the petite mouth of the young trout. "Besides, you don't want to grab it around the body. They can wiggle their way free, and those fins have sharp quills in them."

"It's really beautiful, isn't it?" Billie remarked as she started to calm down.

"Yeah, they really are colorful fish," answered Joey, pointing out the spots on its silvery back.

Then Joey crouched down and released it back into the quiet pool by the big stone at their feet and watched it swim slowly away and then dart into the blackness of the deeper water.

"Holy, that was really fun! This place is so cool! Can I try again?"

"Sure," answered Joey, amused by the widened eyes and intent look on her face.

Joey moved up on the bank and lay down on his side watching her and enjoying every minute of pleasure this new-found activity was bringing her. Each time she would catch a little fish he would get up, unhook it from the treble hook of the spinner, and they would examine it before he released it gently back into its watery world. It was probably 5 crappies and two sunfishes later when she finally turned the pole back over to Joey. Joey was having more fun watching her than fishing himself, so he insisted that she continue. After a couple more small fish, she wound up the line and they sat together on the flat rock and just talked.

"Hey, Joey, don't you ever wonder where all this came from?" asked Billie, hypnotized by the flowing water at her feet.

"Yeah, I know exactly what you mean. It seems too amazing to have just appeared here." Joey agreed.

"I know, right? You can take all the geology classes you want, and you can understand the science behind it but it's just too big and beautiful. It's like when you look up at the moon and stars at night, you can't fathom it. I'm not sure that I believe there is a god, but it makes you really wonder!"

"That's crazy at night! I mean when you look up and see those tiny little pieces of light and then you have to wrap your head around the fact that they could be planets, moons or suns many times bigger than the planet we live on. That's when I start thinking about how small we are in comparison... its totally mind-blowing!" Joey exclaimed making an explosion sound.

"Do you think there is a God Joey?" Billie asked, seriously.

"I don't know. I guess I'm like you on that. But something has to be the source, you know?

"Exactly. Hey, Joey, are you hungry?" Billie abruptly changed the subject.

"Sure, I could eat." Then an idea struck him. "Hey, I know a great spot for a picnic! Just let me stash my fishing stuff back here behind the tree."

Joey led her up away from the stream to the hilltop and the home of the giant beech tree. They spread the quilt over the soft wild grass and sat cross-legged eating their lunches and talking almost nonstop. Billie had made up some tuna sandwiches and for some reason they tasted way better here than anywhere else possible. After the food was gone, they took off their shoes and lay facing each other on their sides sipping coke and propping their heads up with their hands.

"This place is so beautiful, Joey! Thanks for showing me."

"You're so welcome, fair lady," Joey joked. "You're the only one I have ever shown this place to. I try to keep it a secret so that it stays this way, and I can come here when I need to be alone."

"Really? What about Jug? she asked in disbelief.

"Nope. This is Gramps' and my little secret...except for this spot we're on right here. Because this is on a little hill, I come up here once to avoid being seen by kids exploring along the creek. You can see them from up here, but they can't see you. I think I'm the only one that knows about this spot."

"Hey, what about me? I know now too," Billie injected. "I think it means something when you share secrets with somebody you trust. It's sort of special or cherished like a bond between two people. I don't really have a secret that I can show you...oh, but maybe I do. I don't have to ask you to keep it a secret because I have faith that you won't tell anyone. Joey, this is only between you and me!"

Billie rolled over so that her back was facing Joey. She reached behind her and pulled down her jeans to reveal a reddish-purple crescent-shaped birth mark on her right butt cheek. Joey wasn't sure where to look, hesitated but chanced a glance to where she was pointing.

"That's something that no one has ever seen, Joey. I know it's not as special as this place, but that's all I can come up with for now."

"I think that's special!" Joey replied. "It's part of you and that's special to me!"

She had no idea how special that was to Joey! The more they talked and shared things, the more Joey wanted to let her further into his private world, as Gramps put it. Billie shared about her family and how her dad had inherited the construction empire and that her mom's family was wealthy too. They exchanged many likes and dislikes from food to riding in boats and even their musical preferences. Joey realized how completely she was allowing him into her world.

"Billie, I have to tell you some things about me too."

"Sounds kind of serious!" she returned, eyes widened.

"Well, I guess it is, kinda. Remember a little while ago we were talking about if there is a God and all that stuff?"

"Yeah, sure. You're not a born-again Christian, are you?" she asked rhetorically, giggling.

"No, of course not but...Did you ever wonder that if there is a God, how could He let people suffer. I mean if He (or She) knows all things and even what's going on in the future, why would he allow pain and misery?"

"I know what you mean, Joey, but how is that related to your life?"

Joey continued for probably thirty minutes, explaining to her all about his dad, Pam and his broken family life. She faced him, ever attentive and nodding with understanding and changing expressions to fit the context of Joey's descriptions. His comfort level had never been higher and his ability to express his situation never easier. At points he heard his voice break up when dealing with the more difficult scenarios. Joey even confessed his guilt about how he had hurt Gramps' feelings. Billie continued to listen carefully to every word. She wiped a tear from her cheek, as she began to understand how much this hurt Joey.

During a pause, Billie suggested, "Maybe it's like a test, you know? Maybe all the crappy things you go through in life has some kind of meaning that we just can't figure out...at least at first. I think that if you experience bad things, you are more able to understand other people when it happens to them."

"Maybe," Joey accepted. "I don't want to sound like I am saying, 'Why me?' but it's kind of hard to understand how people deserve the hand they are dealt."

"You ever think about 'karma', Joey?"

"You mean like pay-back?"

"Yeah, but a little deeper than that. In Sociology class the other day, we were talking about reincarnation and karma. Some people think that we are placed in this world according to what we experienced in a past life."

"Woah, that's deep for a simple hick town guy like me! But weirdly, I have thought about that very thing."

"Believe me Joey, you are far from simple!"

"You mean like, maybe I was like my father in a past life and now I'm paying for it in this life?"

"Yes. Who knows, really. It might be just fantasy and a way to justify things. The idea that a baby could be born with a severe handicap, you know. It's hard to explain unless you have some kind of theory to fall back on, I guess."

Joey reached down and grabbed his sneakers, turned onto his back and shoved them under his head for a pillow. He stared up through the branches and leaves of the great tree into the light blue beyond. This kind of a conversation was like something he had never experienced or even known possible for that matter. They both lay side by side saying very little for the next few minutes soothed by the cooling air produced by the shade. This place was so agreeable and relaxing! Little shafts of sunlight beamed through on them as the leaves twisted and flickered in the breeze with a soft rustling, and the discordant shrill of a cicada crescendoed and faded from high in the canopy. They lay there staring straight up into their living umbrella, each wondering what the other might say next.

Billie scooched over to Joey and rested her arm across his chest lying face-down with her head on his shoulder. He reached under her and tenderly put his arm around her back.

"I'm so sorry, Joey!"

"Well, I just thought you should know what kind of a loser you're getting' mixed up with." Joey answered in a masked chuckle, rather ashamed.

Billie propped herself up on her elbow and stared down into Joey's face. "Don't you ever say that about yourself! You are the most beautiful person I know!" She lay back down snuggling into Joey's side.

Joey was really struck by that comment. He could not imagine a girl describing a guy as "beautiful", especially not him. The deeper meaning was not lost to him, though. He knew that she was looking inward and could see something sensitive and kindly about his spiritual being. The feeling of her body laying close to him was stirring feelings never felt before. It was not a feeling of lust or just an awakening libido. It felt sensual, yes, but so much more. Joey's heart was so full that he could almost not hold back the tears…tears of joy…tears of relief…tears in knowing that someone cared! He felt his chest pulsate as he felt the urge to actually cry. Then Billie leaned back up to face him.

"And you better go over and talk to your Grandad. You probably mean more to him than anyone in the world!"

"You're right. I will." Joey replied, submissively.

Billie moved in tightly to Joey, their arms wrapped around each other. Joey felt wonderful! She burrowed her head under Joey's chin.

"Just remember who you are," Joey whispered, still staring up through the branches.

"What?" Billie crossed her arms on Joey's chest and studied his eyes.

Joey released his skyward gaze and looked into Billie's eyes. "Just remember who you are... It's just a saying. You made me think of Gramps. He says it all the time, especially when he knows something's bothering me. I guess right now I'm kinda glad to be who I am. You make me feel so much better about everything, Billie!"

Billie's eyes narrowed into one big twinkling wink and pulled her face up close to Joey's. Then she offered a kiss and Joey accepted it, her lips so soft and moist. Joey reached both hands around her body and hugged her lovingly. They lay there, mouths locked and embraced soaking in each other's intimacy and the wonder of the moment. Joey reached further down Billie's back and felt her hand reach behind restraining Joey's advance.

"Not yet, lover boy!"

"Okay," Joey blushed as he soaked in her infectious smile.

They kissed deeply again, and Billie moved down resting her head on his chest. They just held each other and fervently savored their blossoming bond. Joey felt so close to her he could not have imagined anything more wonderful! He thought of how lucky he was at that moment and how completely unworthy he was of her affection.

"Joey," Billie squeezed his shoulders tightly.

"Yeah?"

"I love you!"

"I love you too, Billie!"

They squeezed each other even tighter and lay entangled beneath the dappled sunlight of the wondrous tree. The joy and the comfort of her body became a part of him. The whole idea of Billie's genuine affection and the emotion he felt at this moment, the thought of Gramps and the emptiness that was so much a part of his life began to overwhelm him. He gazed up into the trees and fought the tears as his chest tightened, ached and trembled now out of his control.

"Let it out, Joey. It's okay. Don't feel embarrassed. Your sensitivity is part of what I love about you!"

She caressed his shoulders and he wept as she held him close until there was absolutely no doubt about their intense feelings for each other.

Billie propped herself back up and they both wiped their eyes.

"Oh, I guess I might have lied to you," Joey said in an embarrassed way.

"What the heck do you mean!" Billie raised herself up looking stunned.

"I just remembered. I did share this spot with another girl." Joey looked away as if feigning shame.

"You did...Who?"

"You promise you won't be mad, Billie? I love her too!" Joey emphasized "her".

"You bugger! You brought Harriet up here, didn't you!" Billie laughed and gave Joey a solid punch in the chest. Then they embraced once more laughing heartily.

Through a smile, Billie whispered, "Actually, you can tell a lot about someone by how he treats his pets, and I know how you feel about her."

Later they made their way back to the bridge and stood under it facing each other. They set their things down on the ground and looked at each other eye to eye, hands in hands.

"Joey, I have to tell you some things. Please let me finish before you say anything." She looked into his eyes more intently for a promise of silence.

A little unsure, Joey replied, "Okay?"

"Well first, I'm having some friends over on Sunday. It's my birthday and my parents are letting me have a little party. I want you and Jug to come, if you can. No presents, okay? That's an order! Don't worry, Paul Sinclair is definitely not invited! It will be kind of a school's out party too, since next week is the last one."

"Okay, that sounds great!" Joey replied, knowing by her eyes as she looked downward that there was more.

"There is something else you should know. I know it's not fair to you, and now it's really not fair to me either! I'm leaving Monday afternoon to visit my relatives for the summer in England. This was planned a long time ago and I can't disappoint them." Tears were welling in her eyes now.

Joey felt his lungs deflate, as the thoughts of not seeing her began to creep into his mind. Billie's face sagged too as she wiped her eyes and looked down again pawing the ground with her foot.

"And that's not the end of it. When Mom and I were in the city the other day we visited Elmvale Private School. I've been accepted there. It's the only school that will give me the biology courses I need. I will be starting there in September."

Billie burst into tears and hugged Joey trembling. Joey didn't know what to say. He just held her close and watched the water behind her become more and more blurry. He figured this day was too good to be true!

CHAPTER THIRTEEN

The next day as Joey rose, sat up, and stared out the window, he wondered if the day before had just been wishful thinking, and the miraculous time spent with Billie was merely a dream. Such a wonderful day seemed muddied by a confusion of conflicting thoughts of both love and loss. Joey thought his carnival roller coaster life was at times really a house of horrors. The thought of being unable to have days like yesterday was hard to swallow. He wondered why Billie had let herself get so close to him if she knew they were not going to be able to see each other. It seemed to Joey that every time his life took a turn for the better an equal and opposite force nullified it.

Joey faked Harriet out by leaving some scraps of food behind the house and snuck away while she was scarfing it up. He set out on an aimless walk along the shoreline of Lake Skogie in the direction of town. The lapping of the waves and the natural beauty again escaped him while he floundered about in self-absorbed thought. He continued along and eventually immerged from the brush at the bridge just inside the town limits. A few minutes later he found himself walking up the lane beside Gramps' place. He looked around the property but saw no sign of him. It had rained in the night and the air was cooler now but not cool enough to keep Gramps inside, Joey reasoned. Joey ambled over to the back entrance on Gramps' apartment and knocked on his door but there was no answer. Joey cupped his hands against the glass to try to see past the glare, but it was too dark inside to make out anything clearly. He rapped again much louder on the glass door until his knuckle began to sting.

"Who is it?" a weak voice answered.

"It's me Gramps, Joey." he shouted back.

"Come in Joey. It's open."

Joey slid the heavy patio door open. The musty air of the little apartment instantly hit him. Gramps was lying on the sofa wrapped in the colorful shawl that Joey's grandma had crocheted years ago. Gramps motioned Joey over to a little antique wooden chair beside the sofa. He slid it closer and positioned himself facing Gramps and observed how his skin looked ash-grey and his eyes were more sunken and waterier than he'd ever seen them, with red swollen eyelids and baggy pouches below. He looked so tired and weary!

"Gramps, what's the matter? Are you okay?" Joey asked anxiously.

"Oh, Yeah, I think so. Don't get too close though I might have a touch of the flu. I don't usually get it this time of year, but I imagine I'll be fine tomorrow. You'll see." His voice was breathy and frail but with a positive tone.

"Gramps...I..."

"No need to apologize Joey. I understand, or at least I can imagine what you are going through. I'm actually glad that I was the one you were able to sound off to. Better me than a teacher or a friend...or your girlfriend!" He smiled and stretched a shaky hand over to cuff Joey's knee.

"Thanks, Gramps, but I am really sorry!"

"I know you are. Let's not hear any more about it, okay?"

"Yeah, okay."

"How's it going between you two, anyway? You still seein' her? I can't tell if you got good news or bad news."

"Well things are goin' real good, I guess," Joey answered wistfully.

Joey was thinking how amazing this man was! There was nothing wrong with this old guy's mind, that's for sure. It was like Gramps was a part of him, which in many ways he was. There was the bloodline, but this uncanny ability to anticipate Joey's thoughts was borderline scary. It was like his mind was years younger than his declining physical being.

"Things are goin' good but not really all that good, right? Up and down and up and down, right, Joey…like a roller coaster?"

"Yeah, that's right. Sometimes I wonder what the heck is wrong with me or why things bother me so much!"

"Well, I reckon that's just part of life, especially at your age. You're old enough to experience almost anything that adults do but you're too young to have any real control."

"You mean like piano lessons?" Joey wondered.

"Exactly. You know, I've learned over the years that you can't ever let yourself ever get too high or too low. I think if your expectations are too high, you can easily be disappointed and if your expectations are too low you will have difficulty reaching your potential. The air's too thin on the mountain top and the water's too heavy in the ocean's depths. You know what I mean?" Gramps turned his head searching for Joey's understanding.

"I sure do Gramps."

Joey thought that most people would think Gramps' advice was a little corny or abstract...evidence for Jug that Gramps was a little off his rocker, but to Joey it seemed like one of the wisest things he'd ever heard him say. He only wished that he could reduce the degree of both the highs and lows in his life.

"Hey, Joey, would you mind going into the kitchen and fetching me a glass of water?"

"Sure, Gramps."

Joey walked across the room into the kitchenette area, ran the water until it felt cold enough to his hand, poured it into a tumbler and returned. He handed Gramps the glass, but it was obvious that Gramps was feeling a little too weak to support the weight of it without shaking. He helped him guide the glass to his lips and set it back down on the end table behind Gramps' head.

Joey did not want to say anything about Gramps' weakening condition, in fact, he didn't want to think about it at all.

Instead, his brain seemed to involuntarily blurt out, "She's goin' away, Gramps! She's goin' to England for the summer and to some private school in the city next year!"

After a perceptible pause Gramps admitted, "I knew there was more to your story. We were talking about all the ups and downs in life but when you add girls to the mix, it just gets more complicated...especially if you love her! You do think a lot of her don't you Joey?"

"Sure I do Gramps!" Joey was a little confused by the question but comforted that Gramps understood his feelings.

Another longer pause...Gramps continued, "I know what I'm going to say to you now won't sound all that good to you. But, well...I reckon you're goin' to have to talk yourself into bein' happy for her. She's lucky to have parents that can give her those kinds of opportunities. I know that doesn't help you much right now. It's just another one of those things in life that you don't have any control over. It's too bad she's goin' though."

"What do you mean, Gramps? You just said I should be glad for her."

"Yeah, you really should, but it's just that I think she has probably been really good for you lately…with all you've been going through. It's like you have found someone you can share your feelings with and a person who can provide you with some happiness, right?"

"Yeah, she's pretty special, I guess," Joey admitted. "Her birthday is on Sunday too. She told me not to bring a present, but I feel like I really need to give her something. I mean…I might not see her for a long time, and I want to give her somethin' to remember me by."

"Joey, you've already given her something she'll never forget. You've shared your friendship and she's shared hers. Do you think you'd forget her because she didn't give you a present?"

"No, way, Gramps!"

"Well, there you go…There might be something you could possibly do though. You could call it a 'going away' present."

"What's that?" Joey asked eagerly.

"Well, I don't really know. If she doesn't want a gift, you know, like one you can wrap up and hand to her, give her something else to remember."

"I'm not quite sure what you mean, Gramps. What would that be?"

"Hey, Joey, you're the creative one...maybe words or somethin'. That's kinda gotta be up to you...something from your heart."

Joey left Gramps' place and began his walk home mystified at the wisdom and insight of Gramps' words. He tried to focus on an idea for Billie's present and temporarily, at least, forget about all the other issues that might cloud his mind.

Later that night lying in bed it came to him. He would write a song for her! He felt like a genius! He had to start right then and there. Joey grabbed a pencil and paper and slung his guitar around his shoulder. Using the guitar case as a make-shift desk he worked away most of the evening, combining chords and lyrics. He began to understand the meaning of motivation as he pictured Billie's face in his mind with her whispering, "I love you!" in his ear. My god...had she really said that! He felt humbled and realized how difficult it was to find just the right words. Joey felt crippled in that department. Surprisingly, gradually some words began to flow perhaps easier than he expected. He credited Billie for that. She was his inspiration. He wanted to sound heartfelt but not too sappy or immature. He leaned back with his guitar on his chest and his head propped against the wall. He wrestled with idea after idea and gradually faded off to sleep still clutching his guitar.

Somewhere in the distance he dreamt he heard the phone ring and his mom's muddled voice. The sound in his dream was just enough to partially waken him so he set the guitar down and rolled over on his side to sleep.

He awoke again to his mom's gentle nudge on his shoulder. He could feel the mattrass depress by her weight as she sat beside him. Sleepily, he shifted around to face her, but he couldn't really see her face clearly. It was an unusually dark night, and he could hear the gentle patter of rain on the leaves through the window screen. Joey thought right away of how Billie said she liked that sound, and he began to slip back to sleep.

Lilley shook Joey's shoulder again with more vigor.

"Joey?" Her voice was different and it frightened Joey into a more awakened state.

"Mom, what it is, jeez!"

Joey was now fully awake.

"Honey, come out to the kitchen and sit down. We have to talk about something important!" Her voice sounded distressed, and Joey could not imagine what could be so important that they needed to talk about it in the middle of the night. But there was that word, "Honey" again and that was usually a grim sign.

Groggily, Joey stumbled toward the kitchen. Only the light from the stove's exhaust fan dimly lit the room. Lilley stood in her flannel pj's staring out the front window. Joey walked over to her and noticed a faint reflection of her face in the window and the raindrops streaming down the windowpane. Then he noticed that they weren't all rain drops. Some of them were his mom's tears coursing down her cheeks to trembling lips.

"Mom! What is it?" Joey asked, not really wanting to know as his heart filled with dread!

She turned to face him, hugged him tightly, then stepped back to face him with her hands still on his shoulders.

"Your Grandfather's... gone, Joey!' She choked and stumbled over her words.

"What do you mean, Mom? That can't be! I was just talking to him...I was just over there! No, Mom...No!"

"Joey, he had a massive heart attack…He's gone, Joey!"

She held him as tight as she could and Joey held her, completely shocked and numb, both trembling, taking deep breaths, utterly crushed by the pain in their hearts!

CHAPTER FOURTEEN

Joey was not fully alive for the next few days. The depth of his loss could not be put into words or given enough veracity to describe the emptiness he felt. The wonder of what seems like such a brief life leading to the inevitability and finality of death felt so unfair. You don't think of death that much when you are young. The tightness in his chest burned deeper and deeper, to the point where he felt anger at Gramps for leaving him. Seconds later he felt guilt for feeling that way, knowing that this wasn't Gramps' fault, but Joey found it so difficult to accept death as a part of life.

Gramps' funeral was on a Tuesday. It wasn't until Joey actually saw him lying there painted and prepared in the satin pillows of his casket, that it really hit Joey. He was gone! As the pain of loss once again welled up in his chest, he couldn't help but notice the length of the lineup. So many people had come to pay their respects. They didn't have enough good things to say about him. He had touched so many people! The pain in Joey's heart was partially eased by the adulation and the pride he felt for having been so close to such a beloved man.

Billie's words echoed in his mind, "You probably mean more to him than anyone in the world!"

He thought about how she had urged him to apologize and make up to him and how thoroughly Gramps had understood him when he did try to say he was sorry. What if he hadn't gone over to Gramps' place that day?

Joey thought how peaceful he looked resting there, and privately wished he would move or wink at him.

Joey could feel himself losing his composure and succumbing to his emotion as he broke down into a quiet sob, "Oh, Gramps...I will miss you so much! I know you can hear me. I will try to do my best to be a good person. I'll will always remember who I am!" Joey's head fell and he sobbed openly.

From behind a gentle hand touched his elbow. Still tearful he turned around and looked into the eyes of the person that he needed most right then. He could no longer control himself and he didn't care who was watching. Billie held him tightly and they both cried together.

"I'm so sorry, Joey! she finally said. It's okay to cry!"

After a long and much needed embrace, Joey stepped back and mustered the strength to thank her for coming.

"You have no idea what you mean to me!" he managed.

Joey shook Billie's dad's hand and accepted a sincere hug from her mom as they offered him their condolences. He watched as they shared the same sentiment with his mom, Jess and Pam who was just back on compassionate leave. Lilley gave Billie an extra special hug as they both cried together. That produced an incredibly warm feeling in Joey's heart! Joey realized that even in this time of incredible loss his feelings for Billie were real and he knew how important she was to him.

Is spite of a longing to be with Billie, Joey spent the next couple of days either alone in his room or down at the trout hole. He wrestled with the void in his heart and found no comfort in fishing or drawing. His guitar provided only a little company and although Lilley tried to gently persuade him to go to school she didn't push it too vigorously. She was feeling many of the same things.

Two days after the funeral, Joey found himself and Harriet down at the water's edge. A few hundred feet behind his house was a little clearing with a flat rock to sit on and some shallow water for Harriet to play in. When boat waves came rolling in Harriet would pounce on them, thinking they might be alive. After, she would curl up beside Joey and sleep while Joey flung skipping stones out into the lake.

"At least I still have you, uh girl? You better stay healthy. I couldn't lose you too!"

Joey wished he could be like a cocoon so he could open into a beautiful butterfly and fly away effortlessly, unburdened. He lay in his bed that night thinking about losing. He couldn't get past how two of the most important people in his life were abandoning him. One was gone for good, at least in this life. He closed his eyes and imagined he was at the trout stream watching Gramps artfully fly casting, while Joey watched with his arms around Billie. He fell asleep wondering if the sun would ever shine again.

"Joey?"

"Uh? Oh, hi, Jess. You can come in." he said, struggling to sit up.

"I brought you something." She held out a little bag of mints.

"Oh, Jess! What did you go and do that for?" Joey patted her on the shoulder.

"I knew you were really sad, and Mommy said I could buy you something at the store. Do you like them? she asked, holding out a bag of white mints, proudly.

"I love them Jess!" He hugged her forcing back yet more tears, marveling at how many kinds of love there were.

"Joey?" Jess continued, as she sat next to Joey on the cot.

"Yeah?"

"Mom says that Gramps is kind of lucky. You know why?

"I think I do, but you tell me."

"Mom says that heaven is a place we all want to go sometime, and Grandpa got to go before we did."

Joey chuckled and surmised how much easier it was for a five-year-old to see things in such a straightforward, uncomplicated way.

"And ... he gets to be with Nanny now. He really missed her; you know?" she went on.

"You're right, Jess. You are a really smart girl!"

Joey watched her beam at that comment, and she began bouncing up and down on the edge of the cot. She continued into a hop and bounced right out the door, shaking the whole house.

Joey could feel what must be his cocoon, slowly beginning to open.

He didn't really know about heaven and God, but he did feel this; if there was a heaven or even a hell it might well be here on earth. He had never felt such love and happiness and such pain and sadness almost simultaneously. Joey had a suspicion that we were all being tested for some reason. He thought about his discussion with Billie and about the afterlife and reincarnation and carried it farther. He thought that maybe his life was to prepare him for his next life or that he had been awarded this pain because of something bad he had done in a previous life; karma as it were. Maybe he had been a bully in a past life and Sinclair was here to teach him what it was like to be bullied. Maybe he had even killed someone, and Gramps' death was to show him how the family of his victim felt. Whatever the reasons for the events in his life he could only hope for better things in the future. He was amazed though, at how much better he felt after talking to his little sister.

It was the last day of school for the year and Joey set off. He didn't know what it was exactly that dispatched him off in the direction of school. Perhaps it was the effect that Jess had on him the night before, or the thought of seeing Billie that spurred him on. His heart was full of contradictory emotions, feeling the obvious loss of Gramps, while also feeling an exciting, dreamy kind of love for Billie. What an absolutely crazy week this has been!

He took in the beauty of the area, stalling as he walked the winding road that took him closer to the water's edge and then back inland avoiding the large rock outcroppings. The mornings were like stepping back a few months into the cool spring air before the summer sun penetrated the atmosphere with searing heat in the afternoon. Where the road came closest to the lake, Joey stopped and gazed out onto the sparkling water. This place was alive, he thought. The breath from the shallow, reedy shoreline exhaled in a form of mist caught up in the overhanging bows of the weeping willows and the lower bows of towering pine trees. The rising sun made the moisture-laden, vaporous air turn into a pale gold, foreshadowing the warmth of the coming day. Joey felt more like a spirit than an actual physical being, and his spirit's essence was an elemental component of the atmosphere in this place. As it lived so did he. His mood was its mood.

As he rounded a bend he came upon Jug's house and was immediately rewarded as Jug popped out of the front door and greeted him.

"Hey, Joe. Man, am I glad to see you!" Jug offered sincerely. "Welcome back, bud!" He shook Joey's hand palms in, and they pulled each other into a man hug. "I've been looking for you every morning hoping you would start feeling better!"

"Thanks, Jug. I appreciate that. It's been a hell of a few days! Joey answered still pensive.

The two continued toward the school exchanging banter and good-natured pokes as if nothing were any different than a week or so ago.

By the time Joey had reached his locker, Billie was already there waiting for him.

"Hi, joey." She smiled sympathetically and gave him a gentle kiss on the cheek. "I have been really worried about you. I wanted to call you, but I thought you probably just wanted to be alone. I...I've been waiting here every day. Are you okay?" Her eyes were so big and anxious that Joey began to feel unworthy of her compassion for him.

"Yeah, I'm okay. Thanks for coming to the funeral home. That meant a lot to me...and Gramps!" Joey felt the tears coming again but found the strength to reach over and firmly squeeze her hand.

He was amazed and annoyed at how he could walk to school with Jug and talk about anything without getting so damn emotional! Somehow, he was closer to Billie in that way. Even though he had not known her as long as Jug, there was an intimate confidence that he had not experienced with anybody other than his mom and Gramps. He felt a little embarrassed at the ease in which she made him emotional, but it was okay because she made him feel protected and safe. He knew he could tell her anything and she would care and safeguard it from everyone while supporting him faithfully. How could he know this... feel this?

Later, they ate lunch together and after school Joey walked Billie home. They avoided talking about her upcoming trip to England. The conversation centered mainly about school and funny anecdotes. They gossiped among themselves about what so-and-so got on his or her exams and how it was good to be free from school. They laughed as they recalled how Jamie Morrison, kissing up to his teacher ripped the crotch out of his pants bending over to pick up Mr. Vanderloop's pencil. Mr. Vanderloop, on hearing the obvious tearing sound, simply said, "Thanks for your sacrifice, and yes, you may leave the room!" leaving the class in hysterics.

When they arrived in front of her impressive house, Joey was again struck with the thought that Billie must really care about him. A girl like her, with her affluence, her popularity, could pick anyone she wanted to hang around with, but she picked him! It still was a bit of a mystery to him. There was something that connected them, and he just hoped that they could be together long enough to find out more about that.

"Joey, I have to get going. We're goin' into town to do some shopping and I wanna get some stuff for the party on Sunday. I hope you are still plannin' to come...you and Jug? she asked, holding out her hand.

Joey took her hand in his and smiled. "Yeah, for sure...of course."

Joey suddenly thought that Jug would wonder where he was after school. But, then again, Jug was no dummy.

"Okay, well I'll see you then. Remember, no presents! Just bring yourselves."

She leaned closer, gave him a little peck on the cheek and turned up the sidewalk to her front door. Joey's eyes following her until she opened the large oak door and playfully waved goodbye.

Joey remembered that he had started a song for her and that he had better get to work on it tonight AND tomorrow, if it was going to be worth giving to her.

As he crossed the bridge on his way home, he thought of how every time he crosses that bridge the memory of how Billie had kissed him under there warmed his heart.

The clicking of a 10-speed came up quickly from behind him and spoiled the mood. It passed him so close the breeze rustled his hair. Joey caught a glance of the rider...Paul Sinclair!

Sinclair squeezed the brakes, skidding in the gravel, and unceremoniously flung the bike against the single span of cable between the short posts where the bridge reaches the land. He turned to face Joey and came at him fists clenched. Joey felt like running but didn't want to show any fear. He knew he was in the right here, and Sinclair was the aggressor. There was nowhere to hide or escape. He couldn't run past him to the left because of the traffic, and it would be a dangerous leap into the shallow, rocky river below on the right. He was trapped and caught between the notion of walking forward and standing up for himself and the shaking, sweating reality of his authentic feelings.

They stopped, facing each other about 10 feet apart. There on the cement sidewalk of the bridge Sinclair stared at Joey, shaking, but in anger, not fear, fists at the ready. The scene resembling some kind of western showdown, only without the guns.

Finally, Sinclair angrily bellowed, "I saw you. I was watchin' you today! I saw you walk her home. I saw you just stand there and let her kiss you. I told you! I warned you! Well, school's out Joe-boy!"

Sinclair advanced like a boxer stalking his opponent, and then pounded a fist into an open hand. Joey knew he was outmatched, and this was not the best time to be brave. Realizing that his life and health was being imminently threatened, he turned and ran back towards town. As he reached the end of the bridge, he thought maybe he could hop the cable and try to lose him down by the stream or under the bridge. With Sinclair right behind him he jumped the cable but caught the instep of his right food and made a headfirst fall into the caged rocks that bolstered the riverbank. By instinct, he extended his arms to cushion the fall and felt the biting of the rocks and wire on his forearms. Joey made another desperate attempt to escape but Sinclair was on top of him, swinging wildly while Joey fended off the blows the best he could. Some of the punches made it through and glanced off the top of his head and some found his solar plexus knocking the wind out of him. As Joey gasped, he wriggled attempting to dislodge himself from

Sinclair. Every punch and squirm moved the both closer to the edge of the stone bank. Joey's head was now partially over the edge of a 12 foot drop between to the rocks and water below. He tried to grab Sinclair and restrict the space he needed to get in solid punches and in doing so they both began to roll the other way down an embankment toward the lake at the river mouth. They rolled increasingly faster over the caged rock onto tufts of grass and roots and down onto the rocks at the water's edge. Each revolution brought new scrapes and bruises. They became separated and Joey knew this was his only chance for escape. He scrambled to his feet to make a run across the shallow rapids to get to the other side. As he began to jump over a rock, Sinclair slammed into him from behind smacking Joey's wrist against a large stone. The snapping sound was sickening and he immediately stared down at his forearm and the protruding bone. Joey screamed in agony gathering up his broken forearm with his good hand. He tried wading across the creek while Sinclair looked on somewhat terrified himself. Joey, overcome with pain sat back down on a partially submerged boulder while torrents of frothing water rushed by him. Sinclair stood up, took a step toward Joey, and standing over him pointed his finger in rage.

"Aw, geez Joey-boy! Did you hurt yourself? I sure hope you're ok!" he mocked sarcastically. "Tough luck, loser! Too bad you can't come to Elmvale School next year with Billie and me!"

Joey didn't understand much right then, as he looked up and revealed his injury to Sinclair. Joey grabbed his injured left arm with his right hand and tried to cradle it in a semi straight position while writhing from the pain. Sinclair looking on, appeared sickly as he realized the seriousness of Joey's injury. Like the coward he was, he turned and ran up the slope they had tumbled down and left. Watching him flee, Joey looked up and saw Jug peering over the edge of the bridge.

Jug cupped his hands over his mouth and shouted, "I'm coming Joey. Just hold on! I'll be right there!"

In a few seconds, Jug was helping Joey out of the cold stream and up onto the opposite bank.

"That shit-head! He took off out of here like he saw a ghost! When I saw the panicked way he was tearin' away on his bike, I knew something was goin' on. Holy crap, Joe…your arm! You need a doctor, like, now!"

Jug lay Joey down on a flat piece of granite along the shoreline. Joey was beginning to talk gibberish, felt cold, and wondered if it was going to snow. Jug knew it was shock setting in and noticed that Joey's eyes seemed to roll back in his head occasionally, like he was sleeping. He knew he had to get him help and soon.

Suddenly Joey half sat up and gasped, "Jug, don't tell anybody what happened, okay? Mom doesn't need this right now and…" Joey dozed off.

Jug took off his shirt and wrapped it around Joey's arm, the tip of his ulna still partly protruding. Somehow, he managed to get Joey over to his house by throwing Joey's good arm over his shoulder and supporting the broken arm with his free hand. Joey was in and out of consciousness and during the conscious periods they were able to make some headway and when Joey faded, they would stop to rest.

Jugs' mom saw them from the living room window and greeted them, frantically, at the door. "Jesus, boys, what happened? Come put him on the couch here."

She left momentarily, and then reappeared at the front door.

"Let's go. We will put him in the backseat."

She had moved the car ahead nearer the front door. They slowly laid Joey down in the backseat. She got her cell phone out of her purse and phoned Lilley to explain what was going on...at least what little she knew about it. Joey's family didn't have a cell phone and Jug's mom did only because she needed it for work and was reimbursed for using it. Meanwhile, Joey lay there fading in and out of a stupor, not even aware of his soggy clothes and runners.

As they headed out the driveway, Jug's mom asked, "What on earth happened, Joseph!"

Jug stepped in to honor his friend's groggy request. "He fell off the rocks by the stream, Mom."

They arrived in just a few minutes to the county hospital. After a very brief triage where even the greenest of rookie nurses would have known the extent of the injury from just one quick glance, he was whisked off into a back room. Later, he emerged to a waiting party full of pain pills, and sporting a big blue cast covering his hand and extending up to his elbow.

Lilley stood and hurried over to her battered son being wheeled out in a wheelchair. She sat supported by one of the arms on a waiting room bench. She reached out putting one hand gently behind his head and another on his good arm.

"You're going to be okay, Joey. The doctor said that for a compound fracture it was pretty clean. He only needed one screw and a small plate."

Joey noticed how his mom looked so distressed and tired. He was disappointed that he had been the cause for more of her worries.

"How are you feeling?" she continued.

"A little better. The nurse gave me something for the pain," he answered groggily. "Mom, my arm's broke bad isn't it."

"I'm afraid so…oh Joey, what were you doing anyway?"

Joey caught Jug's eye and he had his finger up to his lips and slightly shook his head as if to say that on one knows what happened.

"I just slipped, I guess."

Thoughts began filtering through Joey's head. He shivered at the disappointment he felt. How could he play his guitar for Billie's birthday present? Did he really hear Sinclair say he was going to the same school as Billie in the fall?

That night Joey was sitting on the living room couch watching TV with his arm in a sling and resting it on a pillow in his lap. The phone rang, so he reached for the remote to turn down the volume. Lilley ran into the room and brought the phone over from the kitchen counter and set it on the side table for Joey.

"How do you know it's for me?" Joey asked, puzzled.

"Oh, just a feeling," answered Lilley.

He picked up the receiver, "Hello?"

"Hi."

"Hi Billie," Joey answered quietly, relieved to hear her voice.

"Jug phoned and told me what happened. He said you fell down the bank by the stream and broke your arm. Are you okay?" she sounded on the verge of tears.

"Yeah, I guess so. Thanks for callin'. What's Jug doin' callin' you?"

"I guess he knows what you mean to me."

Joey's eyes were once again welling. It was as if his heart was hearing her and not just his ears.

She continued, "He thought you might be embarrassed on Sunday, showin' up with a cast on your arm...he's a good friend, Joey."

"Yeah, he sure is." Joey answered, swallowing the lump in his throat.

Joey was thankful that Jug had honored his request to hide the truth about the incident.

"Billie, I gotta ask you about somethin'." He paused to find the right words.

"What is it, Joey?"

"It's about you goin' to that private school next year."

"Elmvale? It's sort of a family tradition, I guess. My brother went there, and my parents think that it would open more doors for me, you know? It's just something the Sinclairs and my parents cooked up a few years ago. I'll really miss you though."

"So...Paul Sinclair WILL be going to the same school as you?" Joey responded trying to sound cool and calm. "I guess that will make him pretty happy." He realized how petty that sounded and wished he could take it back.

"Joey, we're still pretty young, you know. We can't guarantee anything about the future for you and me."

Joey felt betrayed by her words, like a poison dart had buried itself in his chest. Her voice did not sound the least bit comforting without being able to look into her eyes.

"Billie, you sound different, sort of business-like or something. Did I say something wrong?"

"No, I'm sorry. I guess that's the way I sound on the phone sometimes. Look, Joey, you know how I feel about Sinclair. I meant what I said. I'm just saying that we can't plan on each other because we can't be together much for a while."

Joey interrupted, "Yeah I know…Only know you love her when you let her go. Only know you've been high when you're feeling low. Only hate the road when you're missing home."

"That's a song, isn't it?"

"Yeah, it's kinda about letting someone you care about go away. So, if the relationship is strong enough, it will survive. It's just me trying to be mature about the whole thing."

"There is something else I really meant too, Joey."

"What's that?"

"The other day…you know…where you took me…under the big tree. I meant that too, now more than ever!" she was sniffing and starting to cry.

"I meant that too, Billie!" both looked through their blurry eyes and stared at nothing.

CHAPTER FIFTEEN

Under normal circumstances, a party at Billie's would probably have been a fun time. Everyone else seemed to be enjoying themselves. She had invited twelve people – eight girls and four guys, including Jug and Joey. Jack Webster and Patricia McCormick were kind of a couple, supposedly, and Mary Lou Jacobs had a well-known crush on Tom Summers, so that explained their presence. The rest were her close friends. Jug was the only guy who wasn't really attached. Perhaps she had invited him only because Jug was with Joey much of the time and she didn't want to snub him. Regardless, it was a good choice because while Billie was running around being the hostess, it gave Joey a friend to talk to.

Billie had gone to a lot of trouble to put chairs on the patio and decorate the gazebo with balloons and streamers. A table had been set up with tons of pop on ice, bowls of munchies and several plates of sandwiches. Speakers were located under the eaves of the house and inside the roof of the gazebo and the continuous beat of music added a nice party atmosphere which likely emanated from an indoor stereo system somewhere inside the Magee house.

The sound of laughter and giggles, mostly girls, would build up once and awhile and almost drown out the music. Billie was busy making sure she talked with everyone, and Joey noticed that she made several trips to the house to replenish things or grab a rag to clean up a spill. Joey got up and offered to help but she insisted that he should relax and have a good time. His arm was still throbbing, in fact, his whole body was sore as result of the fall, the tumble down the slope, and the punches from Sinclair, so it wasn't an imposition for him to go back and sit down.

He retook his position beside Jug and pretended to smile every time she looked his way. There was something that made Joey uneasy. He couldn't just relax, and he couldn't be the easy, casual guy he usually was when things were fine in his world. Something loomed over him, like a storm cloud about to unleash its fury.

Eventually he was forced into a grin by some of the stunts of the other more extroverted kids. Jack was pretending to be drunk and he stumbled around running into chairs and falling flat on his butt on the deck as he faked like he missed his chair. That sent howls throughout the group and Jug slapped his thigh and let out a few whoops of his own. Joey was beginning to feel the tension release and find their antics entertaining, until the vivid memories of his dad's own real-life drunkenness crept into his mind. He tried to shake off these thoughts. This was a birthday party for Billie, a person he cared about, and nothing should bring her down today. He tried to keep himself from thinking about gloomy things, but it wasn't easy.

"Jug, why don't you ask Janet to dance?" Joey teased, watching Tom and Mary Lou embraced in a slow dance.

"Yeah, right, Joe! Give me a break!" he groaned. "Why don't you ask Billie? I thought you'd be all over her today. She's leavin' tomorrow, isn't she?"

"Yeah, I guess she is." Joey felt sickened by the thought.

Billie came over to the bench, sat down beside Joey and leaned ahead to talk to them both.

"You guys need anything...some food or something?"

"Uh, no thanks," Jug answered.

Joey felt any dark thoughts disappear as Billie rested her hand on his leg.

"Me neither, thanks," Joey added.

Billie gave Joey that special little sparkle from her eyes. He wanted to wrap his arms around her but instead he said, "I wouldn't mind a dance though?" Joey turned to Jug winking and caught Jug's grin and thumbs up.

They started dancing to a slow love song, but neither was paying attention to what it was. Joey's sling was acting like a barrier between them, and not particularly comfortable to either one. Joey tried to keep it from hitting Billie in the chest and Billie was the recipient of a few awkward jabs to her breast. Billie stepped back and eased Joey's arm out of the sling and moved in for a closer, more affectionate cuddle. Joey slipped his good arm around her back and supported the injured one. They both felt exquisitely comfortable in each other's arms as they swayed to the music.

"This party's not quite as much fun as I thought it would be," she said quietly.

"What do you mean?" Joey asked, afraid that it was his glum appearance that made her sad.

Joey tilted his head downward and felt her soft hair against his cheek and was enveloped by her wonderful smell.

"I'm really going to miss you. I think you are my best friend, Joey!" she clutched him trembling.

"I'm really going to miss you too!" Joey whispered and tightened his grip around her. "I wish there was something I could do to make you stay!"

"I guess we're just not quite old enough to run our own lives yet," she answered, softly. She looked up into Joey's eyes, both with tears. Joey wanted to hang on to her forever!

Privately, Joey wished that Sinclair could see them now! Any jealousy or doubt Joey may have had felt completely vanished.

"Well, Maybe someday..."

"Yeah, maybe someday," she answered. "I do have a kind of surprise for you before I go."

"That's kind of cool because I have something for you too. What time do you leave tomorrow?"

"My flight leaves at five o'clock from the city airport. I'm supposed to be ready by three."

"Do you think we could meet...privately...just for a while tomorrow?"

"I would really like that, Joey. I'm still not completely packed, though, and I have to clean up this mess tonight."

Joey jumped in, "I'll help you, and maybe I can talk Jug into helping too...I want to see you...alone. I was thinking...at our spot...the only one you and I know about. Do you think you could be there tomorrow morning around ten...or a little later if you need the time?

"I will try. If I don't make it, it won't be because I didn't try or want to, okay? Of course, any girl that knows she's going to get a surprise from her...BOYFRIEND...would be crazy not to show up, right? Especially when I have a little surprise to trade...one of them you can't wrap up in paper and ribbons, though."

"I liked the sound of that."

"What, boyfriend, or that I have two surprises?"

"Both, but especially boyfriend...and you can't wrap my surprise up either. Wait, I get two presents? Sweet!" They both laughed.

Joey and Jug both stayed until everyone had left. They carried in the chairs that were kept in the boathouse and, of course, were sidetracked admiring Billie's dad's Donzi moored inside.

"Man, that thing must fly!" Jug blurted out.

"Yeah, it probably does," answered Joey, obviously preoccupied.

They cleaned up all the garbage and took down the decorations. When they were almost finished, Joey took Jug down to the swampy thicket at the shore behind the boathouse and showed him Billie's little rowboat. Then Billie appeared to say goodbye.

"Thanks a lot, you guys. You sure saved me a lot of work."

She threw her arm around Joey and leaned against his shoulder.

"Aw, that's alright. Thanks for the nice party," Jug said. "And happy birthday, Billie!"

Billie stepped in front of Joey and gave Jug a big hug. "Thanks, Jug. You watch out for this guy for me will ya? And catch a few speckled trout for me too. You got that?" She stepped back and cuffed his shoulder.

"Yes sir, Mam," Jug joked. Then he pointed to Joey. I'll meet you in the park when you are ready to walk home. Don't get too mushy now!" He laughed, and disappeared on the path through the willowy bushes of the lakeshore.

Billie turned and took Joey's bad arm in her hands. She slipped two fingers inside the cast and gently massaged the skin underneath.

"I'm so sorry about your arm, Joey. I know how it happened. Paul phoned me last night wishing me a happy birthday, but it was just to cover his butt and see if he could be invited to the party. I lied and told him I was just having a few girls over. That was weak on my part. I should have told him the truth. I knew the main reason he called was to make up some kind of excuse before the truth came out about your arm. He told me that he beat you in a wrestling match. My dad was coming home the other day and saw Paul chasing you and causing you to fall into the rocks at the bridge. He couldn't stop because of the traffic but he asked me about it when he got home. Dad promised me he wouldn't tell anyone else, but he was almost as mad at Paul as I was. So, it wasn't hard to put two and two together."

"I'm sorry. I should have told you the truth about it, but I didn't want anyone to know that Sinclair did this to me!"

"I know that, Joey. That's why I pretended not to know what really happened. You don't need to be sorry or embarrassed. You could have used that to try to make me feel sorry for you... which I do...but you didn't ask me for pity. It only makes me love you more...I really do, you know!"

Joey hugged her as tight as he could with one arm.

"I love you too, but don't be sayin' goodbye now. I'll see you tomorrow, okay?"

"No guarantees, Joey. I'll try."

"Happy birthday, Billie!"

Billie reached up and held Joey's head in both hands and they exchanged a big juicy kiss. She turned and walked quickly back to her yard.

Joey met Jug at the bench in the park and they walked home together. They stopped for a few minutes in front of Joey's house. Joey mentioned that Lilley had gotten a full-time job at the Old Country Store and that it looked like piano lessons were once again looming on the horizon. They made a pact to meet by the bridge every other day during the holidays to hang out or do some fishing.

As they parted and Jug was almost in the door, Joey turned and in a loud voice said, "Jug?"

With one hand on the door handle, Jug spun back to face Joey. "Yeah?"

Joey had just one word, "Thanks!"

Puzzled at first but understanding completely, there was a short pause, "You got it, man."

That night, while lying in bed waiting desperately for sleep to set in, Jocy tried to push all that was too heavy to handle out of his mind. Of course, waiting desperately for sleep doesn't usually work. He felt like a small child on Christmas Eve, wondering if the night would ever be over. So much to occupy one's mind! Sleeping should be electronic so you can just switch from awake to sleep. He tried to become part of the waves lapping against the rocks and the winds whispering through the pines that he heard through his window.

"The wonder of it all," he thought. "Why did humans have all these emotions? What good were some of them anyway? Sadness, hate, greed even jealousy were not useful, constructive things to feel. Wait, I was supposed to push the negativity away so I could just concentrate on the good things and maybe get some sleep. There was Gramps but he was gone now. There was Mom and she would always be there for me. But she is hurting because of Dad and Pam. I want to love Dad, but I can't right now. I think Pam will be alright if she gets the help she needs. There's Billie. I really do love her and that scares me because soon she will be gone too. How do I not think of doom and gloom when all the good things have bad things attached to them? Maybe Harriet and Jug...just two faithful friends are actually the best things in my life. I wonder if Billie will make it tomorr......"

After such an exhausting and exhilarating day, sometimes the body says, "Enough is enough. I need my rest!"

Mouth open...snoring ensues.

CHAPTER SIXTEEN

Joey walked up the narrow path beside the trout stream about an hour earlier than he probably needed to. It was a perfect morning, still and sunny with a cacophony of bird songs and a gentle breeze that barely stirred the leaves and made a gentle, whirring sound, higher in the pines. It was a bittersweet day for Joey, and he thought that maybe he had built this relationship up to be more than it really was. They were both young and so much was yet to happen in their lives, he thought. There was still some dew on the grass and Joey could feel his bare ankles getting wet as his feet squeaked when they shifted in his sandals. The level of the stream was already lower than the last time he was here with Billie. By the end of the summer, it will be just a trickle, but easier to catch speckled trout when they sought cover under the overhanging banks in the pools dug from the rushing water earlier in the year. The subtle background sounds were the perfect background for his thoughts and state of mind, for he was at one with this place, body, and soul. He was not quite as anxious as he thought he would be, and he attributed that to the relaxing environment of this stream. Even the deepening sounds of the bullfrogs were more tranquil and less shrill than they were a few weeks ago, when they were tiny.

His thoughts went to a picture in his mind of Billie, so pretty, so kind and wonderful! Then a slight uneasiness crept into his musing; that maybe she wouldn't be able to get away. If she couldn't, he would go right over there to her house. No matter what, he would see her today. He smiled at the words Billie had used, quite strangely really, to describe a guy. She had told him he was beautiful. To Joey, Billie was the beautiful one, but it was somehow very pleasing to be referred to in that way as long as it was coming from her.

As he reached the giant beech tree, he recalled vividly how wonderful their day had been there a short while ago. He climbed up the hill, pushing the young saplings aside while holding his sling so it didn't bump around too much. To his amazement, she was already there lying on her side propped up by one arm and writing something. She quickly put the paper away into her backpack and stood up as a twig snapped under Joey's foot.

They stood there embracing each other with no need for words for several minutes.

Joey unhooked his sling and pulled her down on top of him and reached around with his good arm to bring her closer. She sighed, slid off to one side bringing her knee up onto Joey's thighs and buried her head in his chest. They were like one small bundle of humanity nestled there dwarfed by the great tree and the surrounding forest. She tucked her face up under Joey's chin and sweetly kissed his neck. They watched the leaves flipping lazily around overhead allowing their bodies to be sprayed with stippled sunlight. They could feel the warmth of each other's passion as they clung together in silence.

"Billie," Joey whispered.

"Yeah?" she answered, while caressing the side of his cheek and running her fingers sensually through the hair on the side of his head.

"I wanted to give you somethin'...you know...sorta for your birthday but more something to remember me by.

"You don't need to help me remember you, Joey. You have already given me so much!"

"Well, I was working on a song for you, kind of how you and Gramps made me feel special and worthy."

"That's so beautiful, Joey! Nobody has ever thought to do something so sweet for me! I know what your grandfather meant to you. To be even compared to that is so...so...just so... it makes me emotional."

He could feel her tears pooling in the hollow of his collar bone. She reached into her pocket and pulled out a tissue.

Holding up the tissue she said, "Sorry," she giggled. "But you must admit, I came prepared." They both laughed.

"You and Gramps both gave me something that is so important to me. You gave me trust and respect and...well it just feels like I am special to you, maybe? Sort of like I was to him. I can't really sing it very well since I need a little more healing time before I'm ready to play again, but would you like me to sing it to you?"

"Oh, god Joey, you're makin' me cry again...of course I would!"

Joey cleared his voice and searched for a starting note. He started in softly with a breathy, tender, almost whisper-like voice.

"Speckled trout in a cool, clear stream,

Seein' you in all my dreams.

You shared his world with me and now you must go,

And I love you more than you'll ever know."

That was all Joey could force out. His throat swelled and he quit before his voice cracked and ruined the mood. He trembled and Billie clutched him tighter, as they became so acutely aware of what they would miss. They both lost any composure they may have had and bonded together in spasms of uncontrolled crying, clinging to each other like they would never let go!

"I love you so much!' Billie managed a sniffly whisper.

"I love you more!" Joey answered back, resulting in half sobs, half giggles from both.

Billie lifted herself more upright to look into Joey's eyes. Wiping away the tears she said, "That is the most special gift that anyone has ever given me!"

She reached over to her backpack and pulled out a little red card and then quickly gathered herself up and walked around behind the trunk of the tree, leaving Joey, now propped up on his elbows in a state of bemusement. She returned holding a small, neatly wrapped box and pushed Joey back down playfully, resting her elbow across his chest.

"I got you something too. It's not much but I hope you will like it and show me someday."

"Hmm, show you someday? That sounds interesting." Joey joked in a Dracula-like accent. "But first I vould like to drink your blood!" He finished with a sinister laugh.

Billie laughed and feigned a playful swat to his chin, sat up and helped him unwrap the box. It was a beautiful pencil sketching kit...one that Joey could never afford. It had a thick pad of drawing paper, assorted pencils, and charcoals.

"You crazy girl! That's awesome! Thank you so much! I've seen these and often thought I would like one!"

"I know," she replied as Joey looked back, puzzled.

"How could you possibly know that I wanted this exact one?"

"Well, let's just say that us girls want the best for our man."

"Uh, what are you talking...oh... Mom, right?"

"Well apparently you left the hobby catalogue open with this kit circled on a page. Maybe a little hint for your Mom? I called her and asked what you really wanted, and she didn't think I needed to at first, but I squeezed it out of her!

"Wow, that was like months, ago!"

"Yeah, like around your birthday time. Well, nice try, but better late than never!"

Joey set the box down beside him on the quilt and reached for Billie giving her a sideways hug, both sitting up cross-legged. "Thank you so much! I love it!"

"You're welcome. I got a couple other things for you too."

"What do you mean? Are you trying to make me feel bad?" Joey half joked.

"Joey, I need you to listen to me carefully. I have tried to rehearse exactly how I would say this but I'm just going to shoot and see what happens."

She had Joey's complete and quite puzzled attention.

"I wasn't fair with you. You don't deserve this. WE don't deserve this! I fell in love with you knowing I was going away. That wasn't fair, and now I know how hard it's going to be for me too! Today is like the most wonderful day of my life! I really mean that! The song...I have seen how deeply you loved your grandfather. I could only hope to find someone who would love me that way. Now, I know I have!"

Joey reached to hug her again, but she stuck her arm out stopping him. "No wait, Joey, let me finish. If we hold each other again it will be game over and I'll completely lose it!"

"Sure, okay, I'm listening."

"Okay, well when you got here today, I was finishing up a letter that I was going to leave for you but, instead, I want you to have it now."

She handed him a neatly folded piece of red card stock and Joey opened it carefully and began reading the contents to himself and Billie studied his face as he read it silently, barely keeping his composure. She noticed how her words were touching him as his lips tightened and slightly quivered a little as he read. She gently squeezed his knees softly as he read:

"Dear Joey,

You have become my dearest friend. I'm sorry that I have to go away right now. It's not fair to either of us. I argued with my parents about maybe staying here this fall but I know that the private school is the best thing for me now, so I must try to give it my best shot. Thank you for giving me your world and sharing such wonderful times with me. Please use your talents as you are extremely gifted! If you could only see! Don't feel you have to wait for me. We must get on with our lives and anything could happen. I will always love and respect you, and if you still love me when I come back to you, then it was meant to be. I hope we will be together again someday, but we can't count on that. Be strong, Joey. Your mom and your sisters need you! You are the most beautiful person I know! I really do love you!

All my love,
Billie

P.S. Remember Who You Are!"

"Thank you, Billie!"

"One more thing, just in case you start your doubting," Billie continued, "I talked things over with my mom and Dad and they agreed to do this for us - If we still feel the same in September, which in my heart I believe we will, they have agreed to come and get me every weekend from Elmvale so that we can have time on the weekends together!"

Joey slowly looked up in pleasant surprise while his solemn face turned into a huge smile...almost as big as Billie's. They grabbed each other and hung on for what they hoped was the rest of their lives.

Later that afternoon, Joey returned to the rocks by the trout hole and sat aimlessly tossing pebbles into the stream. This time he brought Harriet along on her lead. There was so much to be grateful for and so much that had happened today it was hard for him to process. There was that pang of mistrust in the whole idea, that doubt that Billie knew he would feel. He couldn't help it. It was the here and now that seemed to envelope him. He had been given all she could offer to reassure him, but she was not here now, and there was no way to get to her. He knew he needed strength to break through the loneliness he already felt. In spite of the fact that, "anything could happen" he knew he would wait for her.

Harriet, spooked by a loud crow cawing overhead sprang to her feet.

"I bet you would like to go for a little run, uh, girl?"

She looked back at him, pulled on the lead and shook her tail with anticipation.

"Wait!" Joey thought. "She was leaving at three and it was 2:45. They could run over to the highway and at least get a glimpse of her and wave goodbye! Joey held his bad arm close so that it wouldn't bounce and took a firm hold on the lead with his good hand. They smashed through the undergrowth and got to the highway in a couple of minutes. There was only one way out of town, and Joey and Harriet walked along on the shoulder heading south toward Montrose. Maybe they had left early, and he missed her. They waited for a few minutes and thought how crazy this was. He felt like some love-sick child, rethought this pathetic idea, and began walking Harriet back to town disappointed.

A black SUV came around the corner and headed out of town. Billie was in the back seat pensive and still trying to fight back her tears.

Billie's Dad squinted and said, "Hey, isn't that Joe and his dog?"

Billie quickly looked up and pressed her face against the glass waving frantically with both hands has they drove by.

Joey looked up just in time to catch a glimpse of her and raised his hand to wave, turning to watch the car driving away.

Suddenly Billie's dad slammed on the brakes and pulled over onto the shoulder, "Go on. Get outta here! You got like two minutes!"

Billie threw off her seatbelt with a clank and grabbed her dad by the neck and kissed the back of his head. "Thanks, Dad!"

She threw open the door and she ran down the shoulder as did Joey with Harriet leading him. Joey wrapped his arm around her, leash and all, and the two became enveloped one more time, laughing as Harriet stood up on her hind legs trying to join the group hug. They both laughed and cried!

"Sorry Billie. I just wanted one last look at you!"

"I'm so glad you did! Never ever say sorry to me again, okay?"

"Okay"

After a very sensual kiss, Billie turned and ran back toward the car.

"Hey!" Joey yelled.

Billie turned, dust flying from her shoes, "What?"

"Thank your dad for me!" Joey shouted.

"I already did!" Billie shouted back as they both waved goodbyes. "I love you too Harriet!" she added.

Meanwhile, back in the car, Billie's dad turned to her mom and said in a sappy voice, "Ain't young love sweet!"

She replied, "I think old love is pretty sweet too!" She leaned across and kissed him, grateful that he had the heart to know what their daughter needed right then.

"Aw gross!" Billie said as she climbed into the car.

"Oh, so it's okay for you but not for us?" They all laughed as they drove away.

Billie turned and watched Joey disappear in the distance tracing a heart onto the car window.

Again, Joey found himself back at the trout stream, Harriet laying by his side exhausted from the afternoon's adventure. This absence from Billie wouldn't be easy, he thought, but it was damn sure worth a try! He began to be returned to the world that he would be forced to face without her.

Once again, Joey couldn't help agonizing over why he wasn't given more control over the things that mattered the very most in his life. He wondered if everyone had to experience the same things he did and if so, how did they handle it? He had dealt with things like family breakdown, alcoholism, physical and mental abuse, drug abuse, violence, hate, death, friendship and even the first love of his life. How do you manage all those things or sort them out somehow? Wasn't there just some way he could just have the friendship and the love? Couldn't he just lock all the lousy, sad things up in some vault somewhere and forget they ever happened? These bad things that had happened to him were memories now, even if they never happened again, all the worst times will always be in his head.

Then he remembered the tears in Gramps' old eyes when he would say goodbye to him the last few times. He knew he was leaving! He knew he was going to die! Joey saw now that even Gramps couldn't control or alter what was to happen in his life.

Joey led Harriet up the hill once more to the big beech tree and carved, "Billie and Joey" into the smooth grey bark with his pocketknife. As he was leaving, he looked back at the flattened grass where he and Billie had shared their secrets. How deeply was he going to have to look inside himself for the answers, he wondered? They scrambled back down the hill, found his flat rock beside the stream. They sat down together on the flat rock. Joey pulled out a wrinkled piece of paper and a pencil stubble from his pocket and began to plan out the first sketch for Billie with Harriet resting her head on his leg and looking up lovingly with her big brown eyes.

THE END

A MESSAGE FROM BILL

This is the part where I thank everyone for contributing to this book. Well, I can't really, because I would have to thank everyone I've ever run across during my life, and of course I would leave out somebody, and likely, many. Nevertheless, there are specific people and groups of people who need mentioning and there are things I need to clarify about the story.

For most of this story Joey is me. His character is/was me. Perhaps he is a little bit you, too?

Many of the things that happened between Joey and his "Gramps" happened between my "Gramps" and me. Since his death in 1976, and well before that, he has been a big part of me in many ways, not the least of which is my love for nature. He used to take me from Hanover, Ontario, my hometown when I was a little boy, over to the Durham area, where we would hike through bushes and fields to find the perfect little stream where the allusive speckled trout lurked along the shadows of the banks. Harold Austin Boettger was born in Hanover in 1889. He married Josephine Margaret Armstrong and had two daughters, Ruth Margaret (my mother) and Josephine Ann. He was a respected man, as Joey's Gramps was, and much more. He enlisted in the Royal Flying Corps at the age of 18. After the war he became president of Knechtal Furniture and for a few years, the mayor of Hanover. He and Grandma also had a cottage on

Browning Island, Lake Muskoka, where I would spend my summers each year. It is likely obvious to you where some of the inspiration for the story's setting and Joey's appreciation for it, comes from. He did coin the phrase, "Remember who you are," quite often, however many think it may have come from my grandmother's side of the family, the Armstrong's. It is absolutely true that his eyes were watery during his last farewells to me. It is impossible to give justice to the depth of his character and what he meant to me, and still means. The lyrics to a song I wrote about him in 1976 after his passing, "Remember Who You Are," are included at the end of this book.

A huge difference between Joey and me was our fathers. My father, Gray S. Knapp, was far from an abusive, alcoholic father. He was a loving, gentle and kind dad, and he actually helped me edit the initial stages of this story. Dad was an extremely talented musician, artist, and a far superior word smith than I'll ever be. I can't help but think how Dad would have loved that I wrote a book! He taught high school English and music in Kapuskasing, where I was born. We moved to Hanover when I was 3 and he took up a job teaching at Hanover District High School, now Diefenbaker High School. Dad and Mom built a house in Hanover on 6th street where our family lived until I was 12, which included my younger sister, Peggy. We attended James A. Magee Public School and I was in grade 6 when we moved once more. Dad accepted a principalship in Parkhill, at North Middlesex District High School, and Peggy and I went to Parkhill Memorial Public School, which is now Parkhill West-Williams. Mom and Dad once again built a new house across from the high school and when I was 14 my (baby) sister Mary Jo arrived on the scene. Dad also became mayor of Parkhill for a term, where he worked on solving the sulfur water problem in town. So, you see, he was no Hank Burgess! I owe my passion for art, writing and music directly to him along with the unfailing encouragement of my mom, Ruth.

I will spare you the trivial details of my life's history, but the year Gramps died, something changed in me. I was with local country music star, Roger Quick, playing the drums for him in Thedford, Ontario the night I got the news about Gramps. As a young man, I felt like superman. Nothing could stop me. But the news that night was the shock that brought me to my knees! That same year I was married and began my teaching career. After writing the song about Gramps, I began to write this novel and share it with my students. During all the years teaching at Oxbow Public School in Ilderton, Parkhill West-Williams Public School in Parkhill, and Biddulph Public School in Lucan, I have always felt that my students, collectively, taught me much more than I ever taught them. This novel was continually edited during those years with my students' input. My Gramps may have been a key initial inspiration, but my students were all incredibly important for my growth as a person and my source of motivation. I remain friends with many of them today thanks to social media. I love each and every one of you. You fill my heart!

I am blessed with having had a wonderful family, one far different from Joey's. With Mom and Dad now passed on, our family now is a blend of characters who all bring so much love into my life daily. My sisters, Peggy and her husband, John and my baby sister, Mary Jo and her husband, Rick, have always been there cheering me on and reassuring me during any of my creative endeavors. I should clarify too, that neither of you were cast as Pam in this story. I have 3 amazing kids; Emily, Amanda, and Will and 2 amazing step kids; Angela and Jon and their spouses; Jeff, Trevor, Missy, Derek and Erin respectively. These unions have also given Cathy and me 15 grandkids! Obviously, there is a never-ending supply of excitement ... and birthdays! How much more motivation does a musician/artist/writer need? I love all of you and appreciate your love and encouragement more than words!

I want to thank all those family and friends I bounced this story off during the final editing stages and especially my wife and partner, Cathy. There could not be a more supportive partner than she has been. I was going to write here that in her eyes I can do no wrong, but that's not exactly true. Because she is able to steer me away from the wrong direction time and time again, we make a great team. Without her constant praise and encouragement and super editing skills, I could simply not have finished this book. I love you!

Picture acknowledgements:

1. Gramps and me at Joey's age – part of a collage, a gift from my sister Peggy.

2. Their secret place – photo, digitally altered by Bill

3. Black Creek trout hole – painting by G.S. Knapp (Dad), slightly digitally altered by Bill

4. Sweet Harriet – photo of the real Harriet

5. Cover – oil pastel by Bill Knapp

Remember Who You Are, because you are important to somebody, and whoever it is, looks up to you. If you think you are not important to someone, then become the person who makes a positive difference to someone else. This life could be your only chance. Unless you are sure about reincarnation.

REMEMBER WHO YOU ARE - BILL KNAPP (1976)

To Gramps

Speckled trout in a cool, clear stream.
Seein' him in all my dreams.
Teachin' me all of nature's ways.
So good to be like him some day.
Always had time for his shipleys,
Gathered 'round him by the Christmas tree.
Smokin' a fine cigar and,
Laughin' with his family.

CHORUS:

He gave me happiness, my old granddad.
He gave me love and that goes far.
I can still hear what he said.
He said, "Just remember who you are."
I think he knew that his time had come.
He hid it from us but I could tell.
Tears were in his eyes,
When he would say goodbye.
And all the people came from near and far,
To see the man who had touched their hearts.
He made us proud of him,
Even the day that he died.

CHORUS

Now he's left us with a happy feeling,
That where he's gone is where the angels sing.
And when I'm old and ready to take the stand,
I hope that I'm just half of the man.

CHORUS AND OUTRO

Gramps and me at Joey's age (14) at the Muskoka cottage.
Nice clothes and shoes, eh?

Their secret place under the giant American beech tree

Black Creek trout hole - charcoal sketch by Joey for Billie on her return

Sweet Harriet